Return TO YOUR
CORE

Principles for a Purposeful
and Respected Life

Jay C. Rifenbary

Author of *True to Your Core* and *No Excuse!*

RETURN TO YOUR CORE
Principles for a Purposeful and Respected Life

©2014 by Jay C. Rifenbary

Published by Rifenbary Training & Development
Saratoga Springs, NY
jay@rifenbary.com ~ www.rifenbary.com

ISBN: 978-0-9832680-2-4

DEDICATION

To my mother Dorothy, whose life was a tribute to the enduring spirit of what it truly means to live a life of purpose and perseverance. Your love and admiration shown to your children and grandchildren will be forever cherished, and remembered for generations to come.

To my wife Noni, I could not have asked for a better person or friend to spend my life with.

To my children Nicole and Jared, you make me proud to call you my children.

CONTENTS

ACKNOWLEDGEMENTS

Thank you to all those who continue to believe in the goodness of others and that a better tomorrow is still to come.

As with *True To Your Core – Common Sense Values for Living Life to Its Fullest*, a heartfelt thanks to Dawn Josephson and Summer Morris for their professionalism, consistency, hard work, and the example they set each day in living the many principles shared in these pages.

INTRODUCTION

W hat are the core values that guide you? When I ask people that question, many are unsure how to answer. While they may quickly state something like "to treat others with respect" or "to be honest," the fact is that they've never really given the question thorough thought before. As a result, they do not know specifically what the core values are that shape their life.

Knowing your core values is essential to living a successful life. When you know your core values and live by them, life is easier. Decision-making is easier. Relationships are easier. Work is easier. Why? Because when your core values guide you, day in and day out, you don't have to stress over anything. When your core values are strong, you know what to do and how to do it, and excuse making disappears. In fact, the more you know and live by your core values, the freer you are in all areas of life.

In my previous book, *True to Your Core: Common Sense Values for Living Life to Its Fullest*, I wrote about the six core values that are the crucial foundation for anyone's life. Those core values are Attitude, Accountability, Self-Respect, Personal Honesty, Life Balance, and Principled Leadership. The response I received to the messages in True to Your Core was exceptional.

This time in *Return To Your Core: Principles for a Purposeful and Respected Life*, I want to take you deeper, to the next six essential core values that will make your life more meaningful and successful. They are Character, Decency, Gratitude, Humility, Self-Discipline, and Wisdom.

I chose these six focus areas for a reason. First, without a strong character and sense of self, you can't be true to what you stand for—your core values. However, when you're true to your core values and display your true character, you can be a person of decency. When you're a person of decency—when you treat others with respect and do the right thing simply because it's the right thing to do—you begin to see and show gratitude for the many gifts in your life. Knowing how blessed you are often leads to a sense of humility as you recognize the importance of others in your life. Maintaining humility in your life requires self-discipline and therefore enhances your self-discipline—your ability to be resilient and true to what you believe in. Finally, when you put all this together, you gain greater wisdom to be more effective in all areas of your life.

These six core values are interrelated. One leads to or depends upon another, which is why it is important to focus on the group of core values as a whole. With that said, however, I encourage you to read one topic per week ... study it, internalize it, and practice it. By year's end, you'll have read all 52 tips and will be a greatly changed person.

For nearly 25 years I've traveled the world, speaking to people from all walks of life about the importance of knowing your core values and staying true to them. With this book, I hope to inspire even more people to embark on the path of living a life that reflects their core values so they can experience the joy and fulfillment that comes from it.

It's your turn to begin the journey. Enjoy!

Return TO YOUR
CORE

Principles for a Purposeful
and Respected Life

SECTION ONE

CHARACTER

I care not what others think of what I do, but I care very much
about what I think of what I do! That is character!
– Theodore Roosevelt

The sum total of a person's relationship to their behaviors is character. Frequently character is the basis for judgment of another. It is a principle that establishes your credibility and level of respect from those around you, and it validates living a life reflective of the core values you stand for and believe in.

Character is defined as "the mental and moral qualities distinctive to an individual; a person's good reputation." How would others define your character? What are the mental and moral qualities that you adhere to, and are those qualities made evident through your behavior? Synonyms of character include integrity, honor, moral strength, moral fiber, rectitude, uprightness, fortitude, strength, backbone, resolve, grit and willpower. Do you possess some of those *characteristics?*

Your character directly correlates with the level of trust you generate with others, and as a result directly impacts the level of communication that takes place between you and others, both personally and professionally. If you doubt someone's strength of character, it is unlikely you will trust them, and as a result you'll be less willing to communicate with them. When someone is seen as being a person of unscrupulous character, it is unlikely that anyone will ever wish to associate with that person. An individual noted for lacking any moral foundation of behavior will not be respected, and therefore serve little constructive purpose.

The principles in this section are designed to strengthen your character and provide you insight on evaluating what it is you genuinely stand for and believe in, and what forms the foundation of your character.

As a society are we becoming a citizenry of less character? Is it becoming more and more challenging to find people of character, who are honorable and trustworthy in their actions? It is paramount to the development of our society, in particular our children, that a focus on establishing good character be in the forefront of personal and professional development. Without continuous character development, immoral and unethical behavior will trend to become the norm rather than the exception.

To be a person of character is a goal to purposefully pursue. It provides you the opportunity to enhance your personal sense of self-respect, integrity, and most important, an ethical example to those around you.

1. CREDIBILITY – MORE THAN JUST A DIPLOMA

Many people know me from my speaking presentations, past books, and newspaper columns. In all of these venues I primarily discuss personal and professional development. Recently, in one of my columns, I ventured away from my usual discourse and pondered a political viewpoint in regard to leadership. Afterward, one reader contacted me and said that I would lose credibility if I took a stand and publically voiced my opinion related to politics. This reader also called me hypocritical for doing so. Could that be any more incredible?

This reader's words got me thinking. Where are we going as a citizenry when voicing an opinion and taking a stand on a belief decreases your credibility? If that's really the case, we might as well throw courage into the human character trashcan.

Credibility is established, or negated, based on principled behavior, not based solely on an opinion. Because a person has an opinion that is not in alignment with yours does not mean he or she is not credible. Credibility is defined as "worthy of belief or confidence, trustworthy; capable of being believed, believable." Being worthy of belief or confidence is established by your character and the behaviors reflecting that character.

WHAT MAKES YOU CREDIBLE?
Your credibility always stems from your behaviors, which supersede your degrees, diplomas, and the number of letters after your name. Having attended West Point certainly provides me with some credibility, but it is my behavior that either validates or diminishes the credibility of attending that institution and the ideals it represents. You can have a bachelor's, a master's, or a doctoral degree in a certain field, but it is your application of those credentials that establishes your credibility. Reinforcing that credibility with a consistency in behavior that reflects your core values is integrity, which ultimately establishes your reputation and level of personal character.

Reputation is defined as "the estimation in which a person or thing is held, especially by the community or public generally; repute." What is your estimation of an individual who stands for nothing and is indecisive, or an individual who is inconsistent? For example, how do you view a person who professes tolerance and then is intolerant, righteous, and indignant when you disagree with them? I doubt he or she would be a person you hold in favorable repute.

Effective leaders take a stand, go out on a limb, think out of the box, and are decisive. Ineffective leaders flip–flop, are narrow-minded, go with the flow, are passive, bow down to criticism, refuse to stir the pot, and lack the courage to act on their principles. How many times have you heard someone say: "I don't agree, but I don't want to say, do, or attach my name to anything because it may cause someone to get upset at me," or "I don't agree but that's not my problem. He is a disgrace, so let someone else challenge him"? Is that credible?

TAKE A STAND

Thanks to the First Amendment, everyone has the right to an opinion and the freedom to express it. However, to personally attack another based on an opinion lacks integrity and undermines credibility. Of course, you can't act on everything you disagree with, but if you passionately believe in a cause, there comes a time to step up to the plate and take a stand. The beauty of our Constitution and the Democracy it supports is that it provides each of us the opportunity to do just that.

In our current political environment, we all should take a deep breath and realize that not everyone is always right or wrong all the time. If your feathers are ruffled because of an opinion, then refute the opinion with facts and figures. I respect an individual who can take a stand on an issue and do it with professionalism and clarity, even if I do not agree with the stand they are taking.

As Mahatma Gandhi stated, "There are seven things that will destroy us: Wealth without work; Pleasure without conscience; Knowledge without character; Religion without sacrifice; Politics without principle: Science without humanity; Business without ethics."

2. CONSUMPTION – THE IRRESPONSIBILITY OF EXCESS

One factor contributing to a misalignment in today's social values is an abundance of irresponsible human consumption. Of course, we are all consumers. And as shared by economists, the health of our economy is directly related to how, what, where, and the amount each of us consumes. But there is a difference between buying what you need and consuming to excess.

What does it mean to irresponsibly consume, and what are the ramifications? We see irresponsible consumption each day when individuals strive to consume to no end. They buy simply so they can have more stuff, feel more important, escape from responsibilities, ease emotional pain, find happiness, or get immediate gratification. As a result, moral decay, economic instability, environmental destruction, political corruption, deterioration of family values, and a mutually disrespectful society ensue.

Consume is defined as "to destroy or expend by use; use up, to eat or drink up; devour, to destroy as by decomposing or burning, to spend wastefully, to absorb; engross." As the British Economist E.F. Schumacher said, "Infinite growth of material consumption in a finite world is an impossibility."

Reflecting on my childhood, I can recall hearing that certain people passed away from consumption. Some doctors used the word "consumption" to describe the wasting away of a person who had tuberculosis. I can also remember the word being used to describe those who drank, smoked, drugged, or overate and then perished from the resulting diseases associated with those behaviors.

On many social levels, consumption has become an obsession related to excess. It seems that many people lack the understanding that there are social responsibilities attached with over-consumption. To believe you live to eat, rather than eat healthy and reasonably to live, will lead to the health consequences that follow. To believe you need more things to validate your self-worth will lead to the financial and emotional struggles that follow. To abuse the environment and the natural resources associated with it will lead to the environmental and energy challenges that follow.

TRIM THE EXCESS

Responsible consumption aligned with healthy and ethically based core values contributes to the achievement of a well-balanced life and the development of a healthy character. Strong core values suppress the need for excess. They provide you an element of checks and balances in regard to how you live your life, and therefore how you consume. Those core values also provide reflection on what is truly important in regard to a fulfilling and ultimately content life.

From an emotional perspective, excess consumption is commonly used as a deterrent for having to take personal responsibility for one's failures, insecurities, and dysfunctions. For some, it can be easier to excessively eat, drink, smoke, abuse drugs, play video games, etc. and become a consumption addict than to cope with the reality of having to be personally responsible. Many use excess consumption as an excuse, and who suffers the most? The people closest to the consumption addict are always the ones that bear the biggest burden of their irresponsible behaviors. Excess equals self-centeredness, which ultimately equals personal and professional misery. The gratification that comes with being self-centered is short lived and lacks any long-term depth of character.

How would you evaluate your consumption? Is it excessive, or is it within the limits of a proper physical and emotionally balanced life? To consume in order to avoid having to deal with a personal or professional issue never solves the issue at hand, nor does it fill the possible emotional emptiness created by that issue. It is a temporary fix for long-term insecurities. To satiate is "to supply with anything in excess, so as to disgust, weary." That is not a behavior anyone would wish to exemplify. As Martin H. Fischer stated, "A machine has value only as it produces more than it consumes—so check your value to the community."

To realize that excess is detrimental to yourself (and is at the expense of others), is the key to being more frugal in all you do. To appreciate "living without" enhances the appreciation of "living within." It is never the stuff that ultimately satisfies, but rather a respectful sense of self that brings wholeness to living a meaningful and satisfied life. It will be, and always has been, creation rather than consumption that has most benefitted the world.

3. WORK ETHIC – A FORGOTTEN PRINCIPLE?

Did I miss the recent memo entitled, "Work Ethic No Longer Necessary"? Perhaps you missed it too.

Have you ever encountered a service experience where you (the customer) felt like you were the one providing the service? A situation where you were treated as if you owed the employee for doing business with them? An attitude conveyed as if you disturbed them because they had to do their job? Is it just me, or does it seem like a strong work ethic is diminishing and that there is an increase in laziness, apathy, and avoidance of hard work? The term "work ethic" is defined as "the principle that hard work is intrinsically virtuous or worthy of reward."

These days, it appears that many people want more out of life without having to work hard for it. This propensity can be attributed to several factors, including a lack of pride in one's avocation, a lack of personal motivation, a trend toward entitlement, an "all about me" attitude, and most important, a lack of personal responsibility. Are we losing the understanding that a rewarding and fulfilling life, and high personal self-respect, is earned not given? Strong individual character is never given but earned by the ethical values you live by.

As in most everything in life, the amount of effort you put into an endeavor determines the level of success achieved. It is certainly a simple concept to understand, yet it's difficult for many to execute. The amount of effort to contribute is an individual decision, and therefore attaches personal responsibility to personal achievement. As Gandhi stated, "Satisfaction lies in the effort, not in the attainment. Full effort is full victory."

YOU REAP WHAT YOU SOW

On a macro level, the most significant contributor to this dangerous trend is the continuous structuring of a Nanny State in our Nation. When more is provided without contributing to the effort to receive it, people have less incentive to work hard for what they want. They become increasingly dependent on the government for their future well-being.

The more dependent they become, the more control and power someone else has over their freedom to make independent choices. A democracy requires an intelligent electorate to function properly. When you take away the ability for citizens to create their own future, the democracy ceases to flourish, and the few have greater control over the many.

I am not suggesting we do not help those in need. As Martin Luther King, Jr. stated, "It's all right to tell a man to lift himself by his own bootstraps, but it is a cruel jest to say to a bootless man that he ought to lift himself by his own bootstraps."

The system fails when those who have the ability and resources to work hard and achieve decide to let someone else do it for them. Such action (or rather, inaction) is a significant character weakness that results in a lack of personal ownership for one's life. At this level, excuse making becomes rampant, and an understanding that hard work is a requirement for a fulfilling life is lost forever. It then becomes acceptable for many to take advantage of the system, because the system allows it.

When life presents challenges, do you take the bull by the horns and persevere through it? Or do you call on Nanny to come to the rescue for every need? The latter does nothing to promote a worthwhile individual work ethic, nor a strong society. Those in power only gain more power as a result of the dependency created and the expected handout to follow. Spoiling our children is no different and is an injustice to them. It sets a precedent and instills a belief that they can attain much without having to work for it. As the legendary basketball coach John Wooden stated, "Nothing will work unless you do."

Yes, there are many who have much without having earned it, but few of them take pride in themselves or what they may have, as it is unearned. Actions speak louder than words. When you exemplify the value of hard work, it not only enhances one of your core values, it also transcends into the core values of your family and our society. As Warren Buffett said, "A very rich person should leave his kids enough to do anything but not enough to do nothing." Rich or not, I believe it is important to give your kids enough to do something. However, do not give them so much they develop an attitude where effort is not needed for what they desire. Of course, what you leave behind includes a lot more than just financial wealth; it also includes the core values and wealth of knowledge you instill in your children.

If you take some time to reflect on your life, you'll notice there have been both failures and successes. Yet the effort you made to succeed, and at times fail, taught you what it takes to have a fulfilling and self-respected life.

4. DON'T BE A WORRYWART

One of the most emotionally debilitating and energy-draining behaviors is worrying. Worry is defined as "a state of anxiety and uncertainty over actual or potential problems." A worrywart is defined as "a person who tends to dwell unduly on difficulty or troubles."

To be concerned about an issue can be beneficial, especially when the concern stems from the awareness that you need to take action to solve a problem. But to worry and not take accountability for what might be troubling you can lead to discouragement, anxiety, and depression.

Life is too short to pass the time worrying when there is so much joy to experience from living. Taking the initiative to rectify a problem is a catalyst for both personal and professional development, and it builds character. To work through what you are worried about also adds clarity to the validity of the worry. You may discover that what is troubling you is not nearly as detrimental as you initially thought.

We all possess personal dysfunctions, face challenges, and experience disappointments. But to dwell on the negative tires the mind, body, and soul. Adding pessimism to worry is a recipe for misery. No one benefits from a "Debbie Downer." In fact, the result is often a pushback from those around you and even those who love you. No one desires to be emotionally drained by another.

WORK THROUGH YOUR WORRIES
When worry presents itself, use it as an opportunity to reflect on the values important to you. Then, use those values to effectively address what you are worried about. Without values there is little strength, and without internal strength worry wins. As Confucius stated, "If you look into your own heart, and you find nothing wrong there, what is there to worry about? What is there to fear?"

When your thoughts and behaviors are aligned with your personal honesty, the necessity to worry lessens because you are being true to who you are. It is also imperative to understand the world does not revolve around your individual agenda. To worry about what is out of your control steals time and energy away from those areas of your life that may need attention. It allows "what might have been" and "what might be" to dominate over "what is now." It becomes an excuse for not taking ownership for the present.

Personal insecurities and a lack of self-confidence manifest the degree to which you worry. But the more you act on the values you believe in, the greater the consistency in behavior, the more secure you are with yourself, and the less you need to worry.

Five action steps to diminish worry in your life are:

- Replace the word *worry* with *concern*. Concern is defined as "a matter of interest or importance to someone," and as a verb "to be relevant or important to; affect or involve." To be concerned denotes a degree of importance and the necessity to take action.

- Be specific in what you are concerned about. To worry each day about your future is non-specific and emotionally unhealthy. To be concerned about the job market is valid, so what actions are you taking to prepare for other career opportunities? To worry about global economic markets is unreasonable for most. To be concerned about your own economic situation is reasonable, so what actions are you taking to ensure your own financial house is in order? To worry about how long you will live is irrational. To be concerned with your lifestyle is legitimate, so what action steps are you taking to live a healthier life?

- Keep it simple. The simpler your life is the happier you will tend to be, simply because you have less to be responsible for. The more stuff you bring into your life, the more complicated it becomes, and the greater potential to create worry.

- Reflect on and prioritize what common concerns you have. Take ownership in generating a solution to resolve those concerns.

- Live the values you believe in. They provide the foundation for effective decision-making and enable greater focus on what you are concerned with.

As Gandhi eloquently stated, "There is nothing that wastes the body like worry, and one who has any faith in God should be ashamed to worry about anything whatsoever."

5. MANIPULATION AND EXAGGERATION – PARTNERS IN DECEIT

Leaders face many challenges, including dealing with change, motivating those they lead, attaining desired objectives, creating a culture of fairness, being fiscally prudent, and maintaining a workable foundation of organizational core values, to name a few. Two primary elements for achievement in any leadership endeavor are effective communication and honesty.

Unfortunately, as a lack of personal accountability continues to fester in our society, the use of manipulation and exaggeration increases. As a result, these destructive behaviors undermine the need for accountability and honesty, diminish communication, and compromise personal and professional character. Why? Because they facilitate excuses. Do any of these sound familiar? "If only you were in charge, I would have gotten that done." "If they had let me do it my way..." "You should be in my corner on this one; I can help you advance." "You are not going to believe what really happened." "It's all politics." "There is no way this will work." "She made me do it." "If we can only get rid of him." "It's always the HR Department's fault." "Don't tell them; they'll never know."

Such phrases are manipulative. They create a practice of deception and destroy the element of trust in any organization, family, or relationship. Individuals do not communicate freely in environments where trust is questionable.

AN UNHEALTHY INFLUENCE

Manipulation is defined as "control or influence (a person or situation) cleverly, unfairly, or unscrupulously." And to manipulate means to "alter (data) or present (statistics) so as to mislead." The primary synonym for mislead is deceive, and deceive is defined as to "cause (someone) to believe something that is not true, typically in order to gain some personal advantage."

Manipulation is tangent to the truth. An individual who manipulates demonstrates a lack of personal accountability, integrity, and honesty. Such behavior also creates a high level of misunderstanding and confusion, since any manipulation thwarts an accurate flow of information. Ultimately, this hinders efficiency and productivity in the workplace, and harmony in any family.

In regard to leadership, manipulation creates dissension among those being led because it distorts the truth. When an issue or situation is manipulated by a few, disagreement and conflict ensue. Some utilize manipulation to accelerate self-driven agendas. If twisting the truth can assist in enhancing their own ego and giving them a sense of accomplishment, then manipulation is the key to that end. The long-term end is self-destructive because the laws of nature have a way of coming full circle in regard to unethical behavior. If you are harmful, harm will be returned to you, one way or another.

STRETCHING THE TRUTH

Exaggeration is defined as "representing (something) as being larger, greater, better, or worse than it really is." Like manipulation, exaggeration also creates a misalignment with what is the truth. In many instances, it is used as an attempt to rationalize a person's behavior or position on an issue. It can also be used to create unhealthy emotion by exacerbating a situation (i.e. making a mountain out of a molehill). Of course, exaggeration can be humorous at times and is wonderful for effective storytelling, but it is debilitating for an accurate assessment of the truth.

One point worth mentioning is to not confuse enthusiasm with exaggeration. Enthusiasm is usually genuine and honest excitement, and exaggeration is dishonest projection. Individuals of weak character use both manipulation and harmful exaggeration as an off ramp from having to take ownership for what they may have said or done. In fact, I have never witnessed a situation where the use of manipulation and/or exaggeration has enhanced the success of a task, project, or relationship. They are always deceptive in nature.

As Abraham Lincoln quoted, "You may fool all the people some of the time; you can even fool some of the people all of the time, but you can't fool all of the people all of the time." May we all make a concerted effort to never deceive and always be truthful, genuine, and candid in our communication with others.

As parents, it is imperative we educate our children in the destructive powers of manipulation and exaggeration. When practiced, these behaviors corrupt the truth and therefore deteriorate an individual's self-respect, integrity, and the development of a meaningful character. If at the end of each day you can say "yes" to having been truthful and accurate in communicating with others, then you will be a person of character and personal accountability. Enjoy the energy and freedom from having a clear conscience. It is truly a beautiful thing, and I am not exaggerating.

6. COURAGE AND SACRIFICE – A PROFILE OF CHARACTER

If you look back over human history, tales of both courage and sacrifice abound. Courage is defined as "the ability to do something that frightens one, strength in the face of pain or grief," and a definition of sacrifice is "an act of giving something valued for the sake of something else regarded as more important and worthy."

There are many who believe that having the courage to strive for freedom and to protect the moral value of humanity are worth even the sacrifice of their own lives. What is the basis of strength behind demonstrating courage and warranting sacrifice? It is a belief in something greater than yourself. A focus and purpose toward a goal that reflects the core values you believe in.

When was the last time you displayed courage? Was it in the face of demonstrated unfairness toward another? Was it standing up for a principle you believed in, even at the risk of your own personal safety or professional security? Was it a time where you decided to not go along with what everyone else was doing?

The strength to demonstrate courage is challenging if you do not know what you stand for and believe in. Without a foundation of core values, you have no platform for consistent behavior, and therefore courage is rarely displayed. When being courageous is based on moral principle and an ethical foundation of goodness toward others, the ability to sacrifice what is needed to make that decision and achieve that goal is validated.

THE FACE OF COURAGE

One of the questions I ask during my organizational training presentations is, "How do you motivate others?" The answer is, "You make people feel valued." I follow that up with an interactive exercise. I select a person from the audience and ask the other attendees to share a characteristic of leadership they believe that person possesses that inspires others to look up to them and to respect them. Immediately they start saying things like "kind," "respectful," "genuine," "caring," "selfless," "humble," "fair," and "honest." But the one attribute I am most impressed with is when a colleague shares that this individual possesses courage. It is always interpreted by others that this particular person has strength of character and is someone you would want to follow when times are difficult. It's indicative of a person who is more likely to take a risk, buck the system, and do what is right in the face of disagreement and rebuke.

Courage is more than just an external behavior displayed, for example, on the battlefield. It is an internal strength of character that demonstrates a firm belief in the causes you believe in and the willingness to sacrifice to see that cause come to fruition. A barometer for your level of courage can be measured by how much you care about what others may think of you.

Do you sacrifice your own principles for acceptance by others? Do you place more value on how others perceive you than on how you perceive yourself? That type of sacrifice is self-destructive because it violates personal honesty. Personal honesty is achieved when how you view yourself is in alignment with how others view you. It takes courage to be personally honest, because each day there are temptations, distractions, and your own vulnerabilities that negatively influence that alignment.

A theme that has always carried through my "No Excuse!" message has been the value of thinking more about others than yourself. The most valuable, courageous, and sacrificial acts have always been when the aftermath has been for the betterment of those around you. It takes guts to stand up for what you believe is right. It is also imperative to ensure that taking that stand is a true reflection of who you are and the values you believe in. Be courageous in all you do. Many in our society, particularly our children, are yearning for leaders of courage and strength of character. Be that example today and every day.

7. POLITICAL CORRECTNESS RUN AMUCK

Political correctness is defined as "the avoidance, often considered as taken to extremes, of forms of expression or action that are perceived to exclude, marginalize, or insult groups of people who are socially disadvantaged or discriminated against." I believe we have reached a crescendo in this nation where political correctness has become a liability to our way of life, rather than a socially respectful and responsible form of tolerance and appreciation for difference. It has become a way to manipulate the masses, stir dissension, and create even further separation.

This social liability was best exemplified in the lack of action taken against Major Nidal Hasan prior to his terrorist attack against his fellow soldiers at Fort Hood, Texas in November 2009. Even though Hasan was a practicing Muslim, I do not believe Hasan's actions are a reflection of the Muslim people, but rather another example of extremism at its best. In regard to the motivation for this attack, political correctness influenced our leaders to be less than courageous and forthright with those who witnessed and were victimized by this terrible tragedy. To spray pixie dust over what was clearly a religiously based motivated massacre is being dishonest. I would share the same sentiment if it were any other fanatic from any other religious affiliation.

LET'S GET REAL

The over use of political correctness has taken common sense to common fear, and sensible communication to an irrational feeling of guilt. There is no question of the importance of being respectful to those of all races, creeds, ages, and other differences, and I personally espouse to that belief. But to not take action in order to avoid hurting someone's feelings and a potential law suit with the end result being the death of innocent young men and women is preposterous. All the red flags were there for action to be taken against Major Hasan, but the fear of ridicule for addressing the issue because others may see it as being racially motivated is the purest example of political correctness run amuck.

Jacques Barzun, a French-born American historian of ideas and culture, author of *From Dawn to Decadence*, stated, "Political correctness does not legislate tolerance; it only organizes hatred." Let us all be mindful of the potential sensitivity of what we say, but let us also use practical sense in discriminating between being sensitive and avoiding the truth. For example, we are not fighting a "Global War on Terror"; now it is an "Overseas Contingency Operation." Are you kidding me? If our fellow American citizens cannot see through this manipulation of vernacular, then we are in serious trouble as a society (or should I say we are "societally challenged"?).

During the recent holiday season, I wondered if, when I was child, anyone was insulted by a Cross, a Christmas tree, a Star of David, a Menorah, a Crescent Moon and Star, or any other religious symbol. I grew up Catholic but never took offense to others celebrating their holiday in their traditional way. It was only when these symbols became a platform for dissension and political gain did I become aware of the negativity associated with difference.

Today, I doubt many Muslims are saying "Happy Holidays" during Ramadan, just as I doubt many Christians are substituting "Happy Holidays" for "Merry Christmas." Yes, I am aware I am politically incorrect for leaving out all the other religions. In this particular example, genuine tolerance is respecting those who may be religiously different and who celebrate differently than you.

I'm sure there have been many benefits to an increased awareness of what we say and what may be offensive to others. But to use political correctness as a platform for power, greed, and control over the masses deteriorates the very fabric of a society that was founded on freedom of speech and freedom of religion.

8. EXEMPLARY CHARACTER TAKES EARNEST EFFORT

A revised version of the Warren Buffet quote I heard recently stated, "Give your children enough to do something, but don't give your children so much they do nothing." This particular thought is applicable beyond children and parenting. It is a theme where the latter endangers the very fabric of an independent individual and society. To be given much without participating in earning what you have creates a false sense of comfort and self-respect. You may have comfort on the outside and a perceived external importance because of what you may own, but there is little internal comfort, satisfaction, and peace of mind when it is not earned.

A purposeful life stems from effort not ease, from doing not stagnating. This is not to say we as a citizenry do not help those who cannot help themselves. However, teaching, mentoring, and setting an example of proper work ethic, resiliency, and determination to those who have the ability to contribute is essential to helping create healthy individuals, families, and communities. Mismanaged and abused entitlement programs are a prime example of how providing too much without requiring a degree of effort and accountability into what one is given generates apathy, degrades work ethic, lessens the desire to persevere, and debilitates any sense of self-worth. It is also detrimental to an understanding of the importance of accountability, self-reliance, and initiative.

To believe you should be provided all you wish for by another person or entity is a catalyst for personal destruction. You can never be rich in thought, spirit, heart, and soul when there is no effort made to earn the life you desire. As Helen Keller said, "Character cannot be developed in ease and quiet. Only through experience of trial and suffering can the soul be strengthened, ambition inspired, and success achieved."

A platform of personal core values is the starting block to transform a mindset of lethargy into creating a meaningful life's legacy. If no core values exist, there is nothing to act on, no accountability for behavior, and therefore no sense of what it is you stand for and believe in. As a result, any character development is fundamentally impossible, since character development is based on the implementation of values.

LEAD BY EXAMPLE

What values are you exemplifying in regard to character development for yourself and those around you? A child being raised in an effortless household will develop an effortless attitude. A child who is surrounded by dishonesty and apathy will be dishonest and apathetic. Children being given so much they do nothing, and expect more, will most likely be nothing and expect less of themselves.

What core values are you discussing with your children, and are you acting on them? Are your words aligned with your behaviors? As Abraham Lincoln said, "Character is like a tree and reputation like a shadow. The shadow is what we think of it; the tree is the real thing." To disavow the need for alignment undermines all principles of ethical parenting and leadership.

Of course you want to provide for those you love, for it is part of taking accountability and ownership for what you have created for yourself and your family. It is also a natural desire to want your children to have a better life and have as many opportunities as possible. However, it is essential to balance what you give to an individual with how you create a level of appreciation and respect for what has been given. To attain a respectful character requires several primary factors including:

- A knowledge base of the values you believe represent what is most important to you to be respected
- A consistency in behavior that reflects those values
- Aligning what you practice with what you preach
- A continuous internal awareness of the example you set each day
- The understanding that character is earned never given

It's time we all acknowledge the important role of fathers, mothers, and family in developing characteristics of a healthy character for our children. These should include a belief in the values of effort, self-discipline, determination, and selflessness, and an understanding that you earn self-respect and a sense of personal satisfaction. These things have never been given; rather, they are earned every day in the efforts you make in the lives of others.

9. MENTORSHIP – AN ENDURING LEGACY

What would you like your legacy to be? What do you want to be remembered for? What do you want to leave behind? Who do you remember that had a lasting, positive impact on your life, and what behavior or characteristic of that person generated that impact? Your answers to these questions will have a profound impact on the decisions you make and the direction your life will take.

Typically, it is never what someone owned that is everlasting, but rather the content of their character and what they gave more than what they took that survives the test of time. Although there may be something materialistic given, the enduring memory created by that gift has little to do with the actual gift and more with the nature behind the giving.

Your legacy is created by your behavior and how that behavior influences those around you. The goodness of anyone's legacy will stem from having been more selfless than self-centered, and having an attitude of service to others rather than solely to oneself. Unfortunately, that understanding has been lost in many powerful elements of our society, and the consequences are evident socially, economically, and politically. So while the majority of us are not in the halls of power, each of us has the opportunity to mentor and be an example to those around us. As William Shakespeare so simply stated, "No legacy is so rich as honesty."

Your legacy does not have to be in the history books, but rather in the hearts of those you have impacted. A social worker may never have a Wikipedia page, but the child she saved will always remember. The caregiver may never get a headline, but the patient aided back to good health will always remember. An ethical and loving parent may never make the tabloids of the rich and famous, but the legacy of the love they showed will forever be remembered and passed down generation after generation.

Mentor is defined as "a wise and trusted advisor, counselor or teacher; an experienced person in a company, college or school who trains and counsels new students and employees." With each day of life experience, we all have the potential to be in some way a wise and trusted advisor, counselor, or teacher. In fact, you are a mentor in more ways than you may realize. And the core values you believe in will structure the strength of your mentorship. It will form the resiliency of your character and be a symbol of integrity to those you influence.

THE WORLD NEEDS MENTORS

In all my travels, I consistently witness a yearning for leadership—for those who have the capacity to mentor others both personally and professionally. Who have been your mentors, and do you wish you had more to help you become a better you? Having my father pass away when I was 11 created an irreplaceable loss in my life and a significant absence of mentorship. It took me years to realize that although my father could not be replaced, I needed others who could teach and guide me to support me in becoming the person I could become.

When was the last time you reached out to someone who could mentor you in an area you are interested in, or to support you with a life challenge you may be dealing with? It demonstrates strength to acknowledge weakness, and humility rather than egotism. It is challenging to be a mentor to others if you are not capable of being a mentor to yourself. To successfully mentor yourself is accomplished by living a life that is honest and aligned with what you believe in and then consistently demonstrating that belief.

Always remember you teach best in life what you want to learn the most. If you have a passion for something in your own life, you will find one of your greatest joys will be to share it with others. We all have a passion for something. What is yours? Are you willing to share that passion and be a mentor to others in what you are passionate about? As William Arthur Ward said, "The mediocre teacher tells. The good teacher explains. The superior teacher demonstrates. The great teacher inspires." Substitute the word teacher in that quote with most any person in a position of influence, such as a parent, coach, officer, or leader, and its meaning will reign true. Enjoy creating your enduring legacy.

SECTION TWO

DECENCY

*"If a man be gracious and courteous to strangers, it shows he is a
citizen of the world, and that his heart is no island cut off from
other lands, but a continent that joins to them."*
– Sir Frances Bacon

Decency is the cornerstone for a respectful and mature society.
Without decency there is decay in the goodness of humanity.

Are you a decent person? Do you treat others with dignity and respect, or do you project bitterness toward those who have more and are more successful? How do you display to others your own internal frustrations? What is your level of professionalism or "emotional patience" when you are under stress and pressure? Is it expressed through anger, criticism, and a lack of patience? Do you tend to be more selfless or self-centered? As a society are we becoming less kind, more insensitive, less compassionate, less humble, and more inconsiderate? Is ego and narcissism replacing humility and thoughtfulness? I am hopeful decency will prevail.

There is a direct relationship between thoughtfulness and decency. When you strive to think more of others than yourself in the process of how you live your life, you will be a more decent person. Decency is defined as "behavior that conforms to accepted standards of morality or respectability; things required for a reasonable standard of life." Although the second part of that definition may pertain to material things and basic necessities, you will discover that it also pertains to an emotional standard of life and wellbeing. When you treat others with decency, it is the right thing to do, and it enhances your own internal sense of self-respect.

What example are you setting, and what example are those in positions of influence setting, as it relates to decency? It only takes the click of a button directed toward your television, or a tap on your smart phone, to witness the amount of indecency taking place in our society. From the halls of government to the halls of our schools to the homes of families, you can witness the lack of decency that exists. What message are we sending our children as a society when we use indecency as entertainment?

The principles in this section are designed to enhance your understanding of the importance of decency in your relationship with others, and to elevate the positive example you set every day to those around you.

To be a decent person is to be a respectful and thoughtful individual. It demonstrates an example of social maturity that will inspire a following of like-minded people who believe in the value of decency.

10. REHABILITATING RESPECT – A SOCIAL IMPERATIVE

Have we lost an understanding on what it means to be respectful and what it requires to be respected? Respect is defined as "a feeling of deep admiration for someone or something elicited by their abilities, qualities, or achievements; due regard for the feeling, wishes, rights, or traditions of others; a person's polite greetings."

It's time we focus on the importance of exemplifying respect. In fact, it is extremely harmful to a healthy social future when being disrespectful is becoming the norm rather than the exception. It completely undermines the importance of social decency. From television shows, movies, media and political pundits to many in positions of leadership, much of the language used and the behaviors demonstrated are shameful. To tolerate such ill-mannered and egregious behavior also destroys social credibility.

The roots of a disrespectful society reside in breeding a culture of self-centeredness, narcissism, and arrogance. Without an appreciation for others, there is no common thread that links our understanding of how to treat each other. The idea of treating people as you would like them to treat you is in need of a rebirth. Fortunately, each one of us is in a position to set an example. What example are you setting? How are your manners? What words are you using? Are you being thoughtful of others? What are your children learning from your behaviors? If you behave rudely and use fowl language, why would your children behave any differently?

RESPECT STARTS WITH SELF

A respectful society reflects an educated society, demonstrates maturity by its citizenry, and showcases humility in its accomplishments. The roots of a respectful society reside in the teaching and implementation of core values that result in being respectful. Humility, selflessness, honesty, kindness, manners, politeness, and attitude are examples of the values that not only illustrate respect toward others, but also demonstrate a high degree of self-respect.

When you do not respect yourself, it is doubtful you will have the ability to respect others. As Ralph Waldo Emerson stated, "Men are respectable only as they respect." To be respectful is to appreciate and acknowledge those who have earned respect through their behaviors and accomplishments. Which path as a society are we going down, and are we as parents, citizens, and community leaders setting the proper example to ensure a respectful future for our children?

Respect is only returned when it is earned. Generating respect is not a matter of the position you hold, but how you execute that position. I have heard frequently that you should respect the office of a person in power regardless of behavior. No, I will not! The office is a reflection of the person holding that office. Behavior is what earns respect, and if that behavior is less than honorable, the person does not deserve respect, regardless of the office. Inappropriate behavior undermines the position held, and therefore the position itself.

However, at the onset of any relationship, respecting another as a human being, a position of influence one may hold, and the life one has led should be part of a respectful society. It is the behaviors of the individual that follows where the respect given initially is deserved or negated. To respect an elder, a soldier, a statesman, a cleric, a parent, an educator, or a doctor is respecting the achievement of those positions but does not mandate respecting the person within that position.

Respect for others starts with respect for oneself. Taking accountability for the life you lead is the cornerstone for building a life of self-respect. To blame others and make excuses for your failures and disappointments in life is an internal lie. You cannot change yesterday, but you can live for today and take the steps to a brighter future. However, it is not up to someone else to do it for you, and there lies the underlining decay in earning self-respect.

Of course, it is essential to help those in need, but when a sense of entitlement is bred by all, respect for self and others is diminished. As the noted Russian author Dostoyevsky stated, "Above all, don't lie to yourself. The man who lies to himself and listens to his own lie comes to a point that he cannot distinguish the truth within him, or around him, and so loses all respect for himself and for others. And having no respect, he ceases to love."

11. DECEIT – AN EMOTIONAL WRECKING BALL

Have you ever been deceived? Being on the receiving end of deceit is emotionally and physically devastating. Deceit is defined as "to cause (someone) to believe something that is not true, typically in order to gain some personal advantage."

Deceit is a violation of the goodness of the human spirit and breeds distrust. This behavioral trait is the ultimate example of human indecency. To take advantage of another's needs, fears, and vulnerabilities demonstrates a lack of individual character that is destructive and victimizing. Homer stated, "Hateful to me as are the gates of hell, is he who, hiding one thing in his heart, utters another."

There have been incidents in my own life where I have been the victim of deceitful people, scams, false promises, and the emotional and financial damage that followed. It certainly diminished my capacity to trust those I conduct personal and professional business with. Being the victim of deceit takes a substantial toll on your sense of self-respect and self-worth. It creates a personal questioning of your skills, intelligence, and potential for future success.

You also tend to punish yourself when you have been taken advantage of, for you believe you should have known better. I have always been one to give others the benefit of the doubt, but that has certainly changed over the years.

However, as with all failures and disappointments, it also provides an opportunity to learn, mature, and become emotionally tougher. It educates you in the importance of being analytical and doing your due diligence prior to making important decisions. When you do not conduct your due diligence, you have the potential for being a victim of deceit. In addition, when you allow emotion to override logic, you open the door to being deceived.

THERE'S ALWAYS A PAYBACK

Although the deceiver may be proud of his deception, what goes around comes around. The timeless cliché of "you reap what you sow" is the ultimate punishment for those who deceive. They will eventually suffer in this world or the next. An individual who deceives has little, if any, personal character. It violates personal honesty, and although the deceiver may gain monetarily or materially from the deception, the gain is without integrity and therefore diminishes any genuine self-respect they may have. As Benjamin Franklin so candidly stated, "Tricks and treachery are the practice of fools, that don't have brains enough to be honest."

How do people live with themselves who deceive? They tuck away the truth, but it is always there to poison their soul. Deceit is a lie without accountability, and one cannot be more personally dishonest than that.

There are those who enjoy the hunt to deceive. It provides a false sense of intelligence and cleverness for the deceiver, and yet never fills the true void that exists within that individual. The noted English poet and biographer Robert Southey stated, "All deception in the course of life is indeed nothing else but a lie reduced to practice, and falsehood passing from words into things."

MORE THAN TRUST

So, who can you trust? That's a great question you should reflect on often. It is important to monitor your personal and business relationships and align with those who share your common core values. And realize that validating those values goes beyond what you hear from them. They are revealed by behavior, facts, and figures.

Five keys to preventing deception both personally and professionally include:

- Do your homework in regard to researching the person, service, and/or product presented. As we have all heard, if it appears too good to be true it probably is.

- Listen to the opinion of those you love and trust. A different perspective is always helpful.

- Trust your intuition and put common sense before emotion and spontaneity.

- Explore the personal need and/or fear you may have that creates your potential vulnerability to be deceived. For example, if you have a need to be appreciated you will be vulnerable to those who, or those things, that satisfy that need.

- Reflect on what you have in your life rather than what you do not have.

Always remember the words of the English playwright Sir Noel Coward who noted, "It is discouraging how many people are shocked by honesty and how few by deceit."

12. THOUGHTFULNESS – AN IMPETUS FOR POSITIVE BEHAVIOR

Before you make your next decision regarding anything, ask yourself, "Does this decision include being thoughtful of others?"

How many decisions are people making these days based on self-driven agendas rather than by reflecting on how the decision might impact others negatively or contribute to the betterment of all concerned? I have no doubt there would be considerably less gridlock in our political spheres of influence if our leaders were more thoughtful, and if their need for self-preservation was not such a priority.

Thoughtless decision making transitions people into being vulnerable to the demands of special interests, cronyism, and ultimately corrupt and deceitful actions. I am not suggesting that all those in public service are thoughtless. In fact, I believe most are thoughtful at the onset of their careers. But the political system has a way of tarnishing that ideal desire of selfless thought and service. Although there may be many public examples of a lack of thoughtfulness, we as individuals have the opportunity to buck the thoughtless trend of such behavior each day.

Thoughtfulness is defined as "showing consideration for the needs of other people," and "showing careful consideration or attention." When someone is thoughtful, it demonstrates a kind and a generous personal character. Thoughtfulness is the precedent for being considerate, caring, attentive, understanding, sympathetic, solicitous, concerned, helpful, obliging, neighborly, unselfish, kind, compassionate, and charitable. These are all synonyms for being thoughtful.

Acting thoughtlessly stems from personal insecurity and what I call misaligned needs. A misaligned need is a need where the outcome of what you want is at the expense of others around you. For example, if the need for wealth and fame tramples those you love and care for, then those needs are misaligned.

In contrast, aligned needs are those that favor the individual as well as those you love and work with, and they possess benefit to something bigger than yourself. Additionally, aligned needs are those that compliment the core values you believe in. For example, if your need for recognition overrides your core value of being humble, then that need is misaligned, and you are less likely to be thoughtful in striving for recognition. If the need for power overrides your core value of virtue (behavior showing high moral standards), then your need for power is misaligned. The desire for recognition and power is a personal insecurity that needs to be addressed before it becomes an excuse for failure.

LET YOUR VALUES GUIDE YOUR DECISIONS

The more you adhere to the values you believe in, the greater opportunity you have to be thoughtful of others in your decisions. Why? Because you are more secure with what you stand for and believe in. When you demonstrate thoughtfulness it reveals contentment with your sense of self and a level of personal honesty revered by most. I say "most" because it can be a threat to those whose needs are misaligned. The threat stems from resisting the necessity to be personally accountable for the misalignment, and that is not enjoyable to contend with. Unless your needs are aligned with your core values, the attainment of those needs will never be enough to reach a level of contentment and personal satisfaction. You will always be dissatisfied.

Thoughtful people are those who generate friendships and family bonds that stand the test of time. They are thinking more of others than themselves. Who does not appreciate that level of selflessness?

As heard in the teaching halls of sales and leadership, people do not care how much you know until they know how much you care. Be thoughtful in thought, word, and deed during your decision making process, as well as during the implementation of your decisions.

The good news is that there is thoughtful, honest, and genuine decency throughout human existence, and it is a joy to be around those who are more selfless than self-centered. Being thoughtful exposes an understanding into your character. It reveals a genuineness and sincerity of commitment toward bettering the world around you. You find happiness in thoughtfulness, because thoughtfulness is reciprocated. How could that not make you smile? As the noted American anthropologist Margaret Meade stated. "A small group of thoughtful people could change the world. Indeed, it's the only thing that ever has."

13. TIME TO RETURN TO CIVILITY AND KINDNESS

As a society, have we forgotten what it means to be civil and kind to one another? Is trampling over others to get to the best bargain really a behavior to embrace? If the answer is "yes," then say good-bye to any moral foundation of decency and purposeful evolution for humanity.

Every year I get more and more saddened as I witness how possessions seem to take precedence over our nation's values. It is this national obsession with stuff that has created monetary debt and moral bankruptcy for many. Although it may be a minority of our citizenry who demonstrate such a lack of civility, it is a trend that should not go unaddressed.

To neglect our responsibilities to one another as a people rather than a commodity is a path toward social disaster. Charles Dickens stated, "The civility which money will purchase is rarely extended to those who have none." Interestingly, during the annual holiday season, we are often reminded that how we treat one another should take priority over the things we acquire or own. But why only during the holiday season? It should be every day, of every month, of every year, that we monitor our behaviors and the example we set to those around us.

It is evident that taking the time to positively focus on and listen effectively to one another has deteriorated. Trends toward personal gratification, self-centeredness, impersonal communication, social indecency, and a lack of self-respect are all major contributing factors. It needs to stop.

Fortunately, there is also abundant goodness and love demonstrated every day by many, and it is the foundation for experiencing and living a meaningful and purposeful life. To serve others selflessly with kindness and civility for the betterment of all mankind should define much of what we as individuals and our nation represents.

TWO NEEDED VALUES

Civility is defined as "formal politeness and courtesy in behavior or speech." It is not only the behaviors we demonstrate, but also how we communicate that defines how civil we are toward one another. The callousness of using profanity or the degrading words used to attack others only exasperates a lack of civility.

Kindness is defined as "the quality of being friendly, generous, and considerate." Civility is much more than just being kind; it is the ability to be thoughtful, compassionate, polite, respectful, and build relationships that foster goodness in thought and behavior toward one another. As George Washington said, "Every action done in company ought to be with some sign of respect to those that are present."

The more you reflect on and implement the core values you believe in, the greater your ability to be civil to those around you. The more secure you are in who you are also promotes civility. As a result, you are less vulnerable to the necessity to behave in an uncivil manner.

Civility and morality are congruent with one another. The less an understanding of what it means to be moral, the less able we are to be civil. As a result, we become a society of freewheeling and irresponsible behaviors with no consequences. Ralph Waldo Emerson stated simply, "There can be no high civility without a deep morality."

Five steps to create a more civil environment for you both personally and professionally are as follows:

- Treat others as you want to be treated, The Golden Rule.

- Be objective in your thought process and focus on the information rather than the emotion. Professionalism (emotional patience) is key in the act of being civil.

- Focus on listening and analyzing rather than reacting and speaking.

- Be keenly aware of not only what you say, but also how you say it.

- Recognize that you influence those around you and with that influence comes a responsibility to set an example of civility.

Civility breeds trust, unity, and a sense of value to those you manage, lead, and, most important, parent. The more civil our children become the more joyous their life—and ours—will be.

14. REALITY TV – DUMBING DOWN AMERICA

Reality television shows continue to escalate. Their dominance as a primary mode of entertainment reveals a destructive trend of inviting the masses to escape from reality rather than participate in it. The public's obsession and the media's promotion of such shows send a very convoluted message in regard to what our priorities as a society are. Are wealth, fame, notoriety, stardom, vanity, and narcissism society's priorities? For the sake of our future as decent citizens, and our intellect as a society, I certainly hope not.

As entertaining as some reality shows may be, they are a distraction for many from having to take accountability for their own personal and professional issues and dilemmas. They also provide an opportunity for one to judge, ridicule, and demean others in order to falsely uplift their own sense of self-importance.

Although some of these shows may come and go, is "The Bachelor/ Bachelorette" reality in regard to what it takes to build a successful relationship? Is "Survivor" reality in regard to what characteristics are most important to succeed in life? Is "American Idol" reality in regard to defining what it means to be genuinely happy? Is "Jersey Shore" reality in regard to the development of positive character traits for our youth? Is "Celebrity Apprentice" reality in regard to the skills necessary to create and run a sustainable business? Is "Keeping Up with the Kardashians" reality in regard to the proper priorities for a personally honest, honorable and fulfilling life?

These questions can be left too much debate and discussion. And of course, you may be able to extract positive life lessons from any situation presented. However, the reality is there needs to be a foundation of perspective when deciphering what is being presented. If no foundation exists, then any individual is vulnerable to what reality television presents and defines as success and happiness. That would be an uneducated understanding of reality.

GET REAL

The foundation to resist such vulnerability is a personal set of core values, real life experience, and an understanding that self-respect is generated by your own actions and not by living through the eyes of others. In addition, life experience provides a basis to interpret real from unreal, and meaningful human interaction from entertainment. What if you have no core values? Then reality television has the potential to influence and form those core values for you.

Related to this bit of pondering is the media's exploitation of the downfall of individuals in the limelight. It seems every day we are informed of those in positions of wealth, fame, and power who implode and violate the very values and character traits they project to the world they possess. A developing belief by those in power that "because I am who I am, the rules and laws of ethical behavior do not apply to me" is self-destructive. How disappointing for our youth when faith, hope, and trust are directed toward those in positions of leadership, only to witness those people fail as a result of behaving in an irresponsible, immoral, and reckless manner. As this continues, why would our youth, or any adult for that matter, believe what anyone says who is in a position of prominent leadership?

Another consequence that emanates from these situations is the deterioration of personal accountability. Every time pundits generate excuses and minimize the destructive behavior of leaders it reinforces the idea that accountable and honorable behavior is meaningless. These are also not times to take delight when those in positions of prominence falter. It is common for many to feel a false sense of satisfaction about their own life when these events occur, but understand it is a lowering of the bar in regard to their own expectations for a better and more fulfilling life.

On a positive note, reality television and the high profile failures we witness open the door to lead and parent more effectively. It forces us to ask questions, evaluate, reflect, and put in perspective the core values we as individuals and parents feel are most important. It is an opportunity to educate our children in what is real, and provide them the tools to develop substance of character, what it means to be decent, and a foundation of values worth believing in.

15. CALLOUSNESS – ALIVE AND WELL

With the constant anxiety in regard to what tomorrow may bring economically, socially, politically, and internationally, you would think that striving for goodness, kindness, mutual respect, and logic within our citizenry would be the norm rather than the exception. Although there is a tremendous amount of positive human behavior being demonstrated every day by those who are more selfless than self-centered, it is always disheartening to witness so many who take delight in personally attacking others anonymously.

Whether it be verbal or written comments to articles and blogs locally and nationally, not taking ownership for destructive personal attacks demonstrates a complete lack of self-respect, decency, and integrity on the part of the attacker. An individual who obtains gratification from spewing a venomous, anonymous assault on another is innately a coward. This type of public ridicule does little to unify a community and its citizenry; rather, it divides it and creates further cynicism and inaccuracy in deciphering potential pertinent information because of the emotion the comment may generate. If you disagree with a person's sentiment and want to express that publicly, that's fine; just have the courage to identify yourself, for that will demonstrate a degree of personal courage rather than cowardice.

In regard to leadership, an authentic and principled leader welcomes ideas, suggestions, and constructive feedback, as it offers differing viewpoints and perspectives on issues and concerns. This provides the opportunity to ensure an honorable and corrective course of action is taken.

The irony with an anonymous attacker is most people do not take their point of view seriously. Why? The attacker exemplifies a clear lack of principled character by not identifying themselves, and therefore negates their own personal and professional credibility. As a result, what could be useful points and counterpoints are less than meaningful.

TAKE A STAND

If any of those I serve disagree with a decision I have made or an issue that I stand for and believe in, they have a right to voice a dissenting opinion and state their case. I enjoy being challenged when it is honorably presented. Anyone in the public eye is often demeaned, but what does it say about our society when personal destruction is glamorized, sensationalized, and used to manipulate the mindset of the masses? It demonstrates an acceptance of a lack of personal integrity, apathy toward dishonorable behavior, and an artificial enhancement of one's own sense of self worth at the expense of others. It is always easier to take delight in emotional ridicule than analytical evaluation of the facts.

Callous is defined as "showing or having an insensitive and cruel disregard for others." How applicable that is to the anonymous attacker. One synonym of callous that stands out above the rest is heartless; and a heartless person is defined as "displaying a complete lack of feeling or consideration." Constructive and respectful discourse is always beneficial in reaching common ground, mutual understanding, and a successful conclusion to an issue or concern at hand.

Five considerations for those who take joy in anonymous personal ridicule are the following:

- Attempt to think more of others than yourself. You will be happier and achieve a greater level of respect and credibility.

- Understand that anonymity demonstrates a lack of personal respect and integrity, and is cowardly.

- Look at the bigger picture in regard to how your words and thoughts may affect what it is you are attempting to make right.

- Ask yourself, "What does it say about me when I lack the ability to take ownership for a destructive opinion that I present to those around me?" Hint: It says you lack a foundation of values that are healthy and in alignment for the common good.

- Reflect on what character traits you believe truly define effective leaders and those individuals who have made a positive difference in your life. I doubt they were anonymous, and likely had the integrity and character to take ownership for their thoughts, words, and deeds.

These are points of practice we can all reflect on as a reminder to abide by the golden rule of treating others as you would like to be treated. It certainly makes for a kinder and more civil community and decent society.

16. DISMISSING SHAME –
A DETRIMENT TO MORAL ACCOUNTABILITY

While en route to New York's LaGuardia Airport to pick up my daughter and son-in-law, my wife and I stopped at a travel plaza between New Paltz and Newburgh on the New York State Thruway. Upon approaching the entrance to the building I noticed a young man and woman, slovenly dressed, and their dog sitting against the corner of the building holding a sign that read "Out of Gas."

At first I felt a sense of sympathy and a desire to help, but then my intuition kicked in and I wondered if this was a genuine call for help. Their particular approach to solving their supposed predicament appeared odd. Mooching for gas money instead of attempting to acquire it by taking some constructive initiative did not set well with me.

After I entered the building I inquired with the general store manager if he was aware that there were two young people with their dog soliciting money for gas. His answer surprised me. He stated they were two college students from a near by State University of New York who occasionally stop by the travel plaza and beg for money. Dismayed, I went to the plaza manager, and she in turn asked the two students to leave.

As I was departing the building, the manager informed me that a gentleman had just given the two moochers $40. I watched as the two students stood up and proceeded to their SUV—the whole time with smirks on their faces. I said to them, "You should be ashamed for your behavior and taking advantage of others in such a dishonest and despicable manner." Their response was what I expected, verbal and physical profanity combined with an apathetic and entitlement based attitude.

They proceeded to jump in their "gasless" vehicle and drive away, proving their need was a hoax and their scam successful. Neither of them had any sense of shame for what they had just done to another human being. This is one example of a disturbing trend toward shamelessness in our society. Consistent social self-centeredness is the major contributor.

THE POSITIVE SIDE OF SHAME

Without a sense of shame for doing wrong there is no moral compass to hold individuals or a society accountable for demeaning behavior. It perpetuates an "all about me" attitude that is completely destructive to a healthy and caring society. Shame is defined as "a painful feeling of humiliation or distress caused by the consciousness of wrong or foolish behavior, a loss of respect or esteem, dishonor."

If you have no shame, you have no conscious, no understanding of right from wrong, and no sense of what defines you since there are no parameters of behavior to hold yourself accountable. As a result, your life is dictated by selfish desires, rather than understanding that a true sense of happiness and self-respect stems from being more selfless than self-centered.

A lack of shame is directly related to a lack of self-respect and a weak foundation of personal core values. If you have no understanding of what you stand for and believe in, you have no sense of self-respect and therefore no respect or decency for others. Why would someone feel any shame for his or her misbehavior toward others when there is no shame for misbehavior toward oneself?

There is also a direct correlation between a lack of shame and a lack of personal accountability. Shameless behavior expresses a root dissatisfaction with oneself, which invites excuse making rather than taking personal ownership for one's life. Irish author Jonathan Swift stated, "A man should never be ashamed to own that he has been in the wrong, which is but saying…that he is wiser today than yesterday." A lack of shame also rests in a lack of humility, which transcends into one's own perceived sense of self-importance. These character traits are always reflective of personal dishonesty and insecurities.

Shame is a barometer that measures behavior in relation to the values you hold dear. If honesty is one of your personal values, and you violate honesty without shame, then violating your value of honesty is hypocritical to what you profess you believe in. Each time you repeat this pattern of behavior you become less in alignment with the person you know you should be. The result is unhappiness and discontentment because you are not in congruence with yourself. As the French philosopher Blaise Pascal stated, "The only shame is to have none."

17. ANGER – A DEMONSTRATION OF PERSONAL IMMATURITY

The inspiration to explore the emotion of anger stems from my sitting on a United Express flight to Chicago knowing I am going to miss my connection to South Bend, IN because of a delay in Albany, NY. This is not an unusual occurrence with the amount of traveling I do, but the lack of concern and nonchalant attitude by the airline employees had provoked my ire. Upon landing, I could always drive to the University of Notre Dame, where I was to be speaking, but the new logistical arrangements that had to be made in regard to my travel and the retrieval of my seminar materials was an added stress I didn't want to contend with. How appropriate to evaluate the emotion of anger at this time.

Anger is defined as "a strong feeling of annoyance, displeasure, or hostility" Where does that strong feeling stem from? Are the roots of anger similar in all human beings? Is anger a choice, or is it a normal reaction to the descriptive words above?

Behind every emotion there is a reason, and those reasons are unique to each of us. We all experience anger, but when it is expressed through abusive behavior that is a reflection of personal immaturity. A reaction of abusive anger to a situation can easily be attributed to personal insecurities, childhood experiences, and fears attributed to what was, or what might be. However, it is reactive not proactive, and a choice made. If the results are destructive, the emotional reasons behind the anger do not justify the hurt caused to oneself or to others. There are times where anger may appear to be appropriate, but when the dust settles I have never known someone to be proud of his or her angry behavior. It is important to recognize that each anger moment destroys a segment of self-respect.

The venting of abusive anger is a display of a person's insecurity, immaturity, and inability to patiently handle a situation. Is a lack of patience a precursor to igniting anger? If so, what are you impatient about? The slow driver in front of you? A lack of assertiveness by an employee? The weather? A mistake made by a child? A sense there is no attention being paid to you? A lack of personal and professional fulfillment?

CALM DOWN

Taking accountability in recognizing personal anger, and taking the steps to prevent the emotional fallout from anger, is a challenging undertaking. With the success of reducing the onset of anger in your life comes tremendous personal growth. It also initiates a significant reduction in stress and other negative health related symptoms. An increase in heart rate and blood pressure, and emotional instability, negatively impacts the body and mind in ways that are still not totally understood. Is getting angry over minutia really worth jeopardizing your health? Does creating further complexity in your life and acquiring more material things reduce the potential for further anger? It is just the opposite, for it creates more stress, more responsibility, and greater potential to spark anger as a result of frustration or dissatisfaction.

Over the years I have discovered the simpler my life is, the happier I tend to be, because the less I have to be responsible for. As a result, the less I have to be angry about. Six practical steps to reducing anger in your life include:

- Recognize what situation is initiating the anger, and analyze the situation rather than immediately reacting to it.

- Ask yourself, "Is this incident I am confronting really worth getting angry about?"

- If anger does occur, focus on whom the anger is directed toward and ask yourself, "Will the anger change the person's behavior or repair the situation? If not, the anger is a waste of time and energy.

- Ask, "What will be the result of displaying anger? I have never known anger to result in a more healthy and harmonious environment. It opens wounds, new and old, and creates a defensive mechanism that generates even more harm.

- Simplify your life.

- Set an example in all you do.

Anger diminishes your emotional stability and reputation, and it sends a message of unprofessionalism. When you demonstrate calm in the throes of chaos, the reward of personal respect, and the respect expressed to you by others, will be the result of your maturity and professionalism.

18. SELF-RIGHTEOUSNESS – THE DEMISE OF COMPROMISE

In the halls of many levels of government, the lack of cooperation and compromise from differing sides of the aisle has brought about divisiveness, animosity, and anger, all of which lead to a potential economic disaster and a lack of efficiency in governing. Honest public service means not allowing pride and ego to override the responsibilities and obligations to those who are to be served. Throughout history, compromise has played a vital role in the progression of human achievement. Agreements, policies, treaties, and doctrines of all kinds have been created and subsequently implemented through effective compromise. Our Constitution and Bill of Rights is a prime example. There are exceptions, but genuine leadership recognizes that unifying the many outweighs the self-interest and self-driven agendas of the few.

Compromise is a vital component in creating an atmosphere of unity, cooperation, and decency. A lack of compromise by leadership sustains a polarization of those impacted by any decision made. Because differing viewpoints and considerations are not addressed, distrust and anger among the group grows. Of course, there are times when compromise cannot be part of the leadership equation, especially when life or death may be at stake, such as in the midst of military combat.

Compromise is defined as "a settlement of differences by mutual concessions; an agreement reached by adjustment of conflicting or opposing claims, principles, etc., by reciprocal modification of demands." Is it just me, or does that definition appear to *not* resonate with many in positions of political power today?

The antithesis of compromising leadership is self-righteous leadership. Self-righteous is defined as "confident of one's own righteousness, especially when smugly moralistic and intolerant of the opinions and behaviors of others." A self-righteous leader is less likely to be empathetic, inclusive, compassionate, selfless, or considerate of another. Self-righteous leadership on all levels displays arrogance and creates division within a family, organization, community, state, and nation. It demeans, divides, disrespects, and denigrates those who are to follow.

62

HOW COMPROMISE AFFECTS YOUR VALUES

To compromise on an issue or a policy does not necessarily demand that you compromise on your values. For example, you can be honest and still work toward a solution that involves compromise. However, there are issues that relate to an adherence to a certain faith or moralistic belief, and these instances prove the most difficult to compromise on. When opposing parties collide, the most beneficial and successful decisions made stem from a degree of cooperation and some level of compromise. The more inclusive the result of a decision may be, the more unifying the role of leadership is.

Any successful relationship has elements of concessions and compromise. Marriage immediately comes to mind, and I have never witnessed a happy marriage, happy family, or any happy relationship that is totalitarian or dictatorial in nature. Such a lack of compromise discounts the value of those you have a relationship with. To reach a compromise on any issue requires greater listening on both sides and the ability to see a practical picture, not solely an ideological one. It requires patience, perseverance, empathy, and a willingness to be objective in the process of reaching a mutually beneficial, fair, and reasonable decision.

Of course, to compromise in regard to a violation of human rights by another person, citizenry, or government is irresponsible and should not be tolerated by any society. It is always the few, the powerful, and the extreme that destroy the many and disintegrate the value of humanity.

Compromise is never to be used as an excuse to not hold people, institutions, and governments accountable for irresponsible behavior and inhumane treatment. There has been, and continues to be, those in positions of power and leadership who recognize the destructive nature of self-righteous leadership, and who work to lessen its detrimental impact on the greater good. Our world would be much worse off if there were not those who fought the good fight for the many, rather than the few.

As the poet Phyllis McGinley said, "Compromise, if not the spice of life, is its solidity. It is what makes nations great and marriages happy." Be a leader of the many in your home, your community, and those you influence every day.

SECTION THREE

GRATITUDE

As we express our gratitude, we must never forget that the high-est appreciation is not to utter words, but to live by them.
– John F. Kennedy

To be grateful is to be appreciative for the blessings you have, and to be accepting of the life you have created. No one, nor any family, is without pain and hardship, and at times it appears that a level of unfairness exists during the course of our lives. However, to be grateful is to be free of the burden of what you don't have and celebrate the people and the things that you do have.

When was the last time you took a step back and reflected on what is right in your life? What are your priorities in regard to what you appreciate? What do you appreciate more, your health or to have more money than the next person? What do you appreciate more, your family or your self-centered desires? What do you appreciate more, optimism or pessimism? What do you appreciate more, the thoughtful people in your life or the disrespectful ones? We may all have different priorities, but to disavow the importance of being grateful is to embrace the behaviors of self-centeredness and thoughtlessness, and what a lonely life that will be.

How grateful are you? Gratitude is defined as "the quality of being thankful; readiness to show appreciation for and to return kindness." How often have you been ready to show appreciation and return kindness? You will find joy in being kind. You will find joy in being more thoughtful than thoughtless. You will find joy in giving more than taking more.

The principles in this section are designed to elevate your appreciation for what and who is around you. It will provide additional perspective on how each day is an opportunity to be a valuable part of something. You will always attract what you project, and when you display gratitude you will attract those who are grateful for having you in their life.

Do not reserve being grateful for only the holidays, but live a life of gratitude daily. It will lighten and inspire not only your own spirit, but also lift the spirit of those around you. When the desire for more takes precedence over being grateful for what you have, the "more" will never be enough. Gratitude is having no regrets and appreciating what was and what can be, rather than what should have been.

19. BLESSINGS – WHAT IS RIGHT IN YOUR LIFE?

In order to recognize the blessings in your life, it's essential to take some time to reflect on the bright spots of your life and cast aside, at least for the moment, any darkness that may exist. Remember that there are those who love you, and those you love. To focus on the negative, to hope for a better past, and to be pessimistic about the future are choices—ones that are emotionally and physically destructive. Life is too short to worry about everything wrong with it. In fact, you will find the more you think of others, the happier you tend to be, and as a result your worries and issues will seem less dire.

There is little reason to whine about what "things" you don't' have, or blame someone else for what your lot in life may not be. Reflect on the past, but don't dwell on it. Cherish the fond memories; don't use what should have been, might have been, or could have been as excuses for what cannot be. By doing this, you will recognize and appreciate the blessings you currently have. You will gain an understanding that your behavior reflects your character, and that selflessness not self-centeredness is the cornerstone for happiness. As Charles Dickens said, "Reflect upon your present blessings—of which every man has many—not on your past misfortunes, of which all men have some."

YOUR BLESSINGS ARE EVERYWHERE

A definition of blessing is "a beneficial thing for which one is grateful; something that brings well-being." When was the last time you reflected on what you are grateful for and what brings you well being? The love of your spouse, the wonderment of your children, the ability to enjoy a sunny day, the bounty of a wonderful meal, the joy to laugh and cry with those you love, and the opportunity to make a positive difference in another each day are examples of how fortunate you may be.

What example are you setting to those you love, and those who love you? Are you shining goodness to those around you, or an attitude of being the victim of everything that negatively happened to you? I believe in the moral strength and eternal spirit of humanity, that goodness will prevail over evil, and content of character will endure beyond materialism. Who you are and what you stand for and believe in are not controlled by the outside, but by the internal choice to live and act on the core values you believe in. It is the constant regurgitation of the negative that poisons the very spirit of optimism. The fiscal cliff, the Middle East, the jobless rate, the loss of personal accountability, the decline of respect, and the breakdown of family and moral relativity are all examples of what we are inundated with each day.

Despite all this negativity, the fact is that the world is not coming to an end. So shut out the negative and look for the positive in and around you. As Henry Ward Beecher said, "The unthankful heart discovers no mercies; but the thankful heart will find, in every hour, some heavenly blessings." Throw out your darkness and invite your spirit of light to shine through.

Blessings are not always given, but also earned through the love, compassion, empathy, kindness, forgiveness, and respect each of us shows to another. Our greatest blessings rarely have a price tag attached to them, but rather a human tag labeled family, friends, memories, and those who gave of themselves to help develop a better you. Each day, take a moment to observe, listen, and count your blessings. When you do, you'll be better able to exemplify a spirit of love, forgiveness, and emotional generosity to those around you.

20. FAMILY TIME – BEING THANKFUL FOR TOGETHERNESS

Over the past many months I have appreciated time with family more than ever in my life. Recently my daughter and son-in-law moved back to the area from Albuquerque, NM. To experience my daughter's maturity has been genuinely rewarding. To have family near is a blessing and something I will never take for granted.

Bonding as a family requires patience, loyalty, trust, tolerance, and objectivity. It also demands discipline, a foundation of core values, and a consistency in the application of those values. That's why what your family stands for and believes in should be defined, reviewed, shared, questioned, and acted upon. It is more than a discussion; it is a decision to live by the values that unify a mother, father, their children, and the grandchildren now and into the future.

Family is defined as "a basic social unit consisting of parents and their children, considered as a group, whether dwelling together or not: the traditional family." There are many variations of families and how families can be defined; however, it is the mutual respect and love demonstrated to one another within a family that is enduring through good times and bad. Granted, there will always be issues, mistakes made, and differences among family members, but the union within an immediate family should display a level of unconditional love, loyalty, and commitment that supersedes all others.

LOVE AND VALUES

To be loving within a family is to be respectful of others regardless of differences in opinion. Doing so demonstrates a commitment to the familial relationship. Family forms the foundation for fortitude. To be an effective parent is to align what you project outside your home with how you behave inside your home. Hypocrisy between words and actions destroys respect, trust, and the bonds that build a strong, resilient, and perseverant family.

Do your children know the values of their family? Have you ever asked them? What would they say? Do not assume they know the answer, for assumptions are based on personal impressions and perceptions, not on a mutual analysis and understanding of a situation. Assume is defined as "the act of taking for granted or supposing." To assume and not ask the "values" question of those you parent and love only creates potential misunderstanding, confusion, and unexpected behaviors.

In raising my own children, there were times I assumed what my children were thinking and how they were behaving. When my assumption was wrong, there were always consequences and misunderstandings that followed. I am not suggesting you should be a "Velcro" parent and attach yourself to your children every moment of every day, but I am suggesting you display a consistency in dialogue and parental behavior by reiterating the values important to your family.

FAMILY IS FOREVER

Every family, like every person, has their dysfunctions. Anyone who believes otherwise is in serious denial. Personal and family development is a continuous work in progress that never ends. It is being accountable for the journey and striving to consistently live the values you believe in that bring your individual and family efforts to a positive fruition. Fun is fleeting, but family is forever. Of course, nothing is perfect and there will always be situations and family conflicts that are challenging to overcome, and at times never resolved. However, it is worthwhile to always strive to build on the strengths that exist and not dwell on the weaknesses or failures that might have occurred.

As in all of life's endeavors, it is important to surround yourself with positive people and behaviors rather than the negative ones, for you attract what you associate with. There may be those in your "Relative" circle who I call the "Dranoids," those who just suck the positive energy right out of you. To be respectful is important, but to attempt to change them will be exhausting and doubtful. It will only be their own recognition and taking accountability for their self-destructive behavior that will be the catalyst for them to change.

Families are like fudge, mostly sweet, but occasionally a few nuts are thrown in. I hope you will take the time to pose the question of family values to those you love. I believe you will be pleasantly surprised, proud, and educated by the responses provided. It will also provide a framework of respect and accountability as you and your family move forward. As Mother Teresa stated, "What can you do to promote world peace? Go home and love your family."

21. APPRECIATING OUR SEASONED CITIZENS

As the proper seasoning of food always enhances the flavor of a wonderful meal, the proper seasoning of a person always enhances the experiences of a wonderful life. I am very appreciative for all those who have come full circle in life—those whose bodies and minds are struggling with a sense of youthfulness, and who are attempting to maintain meaning to the many marvelous memories of the past while applying their life lessons to the present. Aging is an opportunity to reminisce on the joyful moments and loving people one has experienced in life. As Mark Twain stated, "Age is an issue of mind over matter. If you don't mind, it doesn't matter."

It is the cycle of experience that teaches the lessons of life. With knowledge comes understanding, and with understanding comes wisdom. Experience validates the accuracy of knowledge and acts as the bridge that connects those three facets of learning.

We gain wisdom by becoming seasoned. The wisdom of our seniors should never be taken for granted, but rather acknowledged and respected. It is an appreciation for that seasoning that maintains a respectful society and a deep-rooted sense of family and community. I witness time after time a failure by many to learn from and respect those who have experienced longevity.

Technology has always moved a society forward, yet it also tends to leave a generation lagging behind. Our youth often discredit the elderly for being naïve to new technology or for making a decision not to participate with technological advancements. Living a full life is more than just being proficient with a smart phone. It is the collection of a life of experiences that culminates into a wholeness of what it means to have lived. To discard the lessons of experience for the possible immediate gratification of wealth, fame, and power is a recipe for social decay.

LEARN FROM THEIR WISDOM
How many social and economic decisions have been, and continue to be made, without considering the lessons of yesterday and the wisdom

of those who have come before us? As the Spanish philosopher George Santayana said, "Those who cannot remember the past are condemned to repeat it." It certainly appears there are many in power who fail to heed that advice. As a result, they make decisions based on what is in the best interest of the few and the present, rather than the many and the future.

What many of our elderly have witnessed, struggled with, and experienced can provide a textbook of knowledge as important as any in the classroom. In fact, life lessons from our seniors would make a meaningful piece of academic curriculum. Learning history with differing real life perspectives might just add to a greater level of empathy, civility, and compassion toward those around us. At your first opportunity, take a moment with a seasoned citizen in your life and ask a pertinent question that may reflect a difficulty in your own life. You may be surprised at the level of wisdom you receive with their response.

It is also disheartening to see the reaction by many toward our seniors because of their inability to walk as fast, hear or see as well, think as sharply, or comprehend the pace of change before them. I hope all of us take the time to be more thoughtful before we judge or become impatient with those in their golden years. Most of us will be there someday, and I am sure you would not want someone to demean or undermine who you are, what you are, and what your life has been.

Capitalize on an opportunity to display respect to those who are seasoned. Opening a door, expressing a smile, acknowledging an opinion, taking a moment to listen, or thanking them for their contribution are all examples of what might bring a warm sense of feeling valued to an elder. It is more important to be empathetic then sympathetic to our elders. Empathy is more respectful, for it is a conscious effort to understand and learn from another rather than only sharing their feelings. It demonstrates a willingness to participate vicariously in their life experience that will be appreciated and respected. As John Barrymore said, "A man is not old until regrets take the place of dreams." Remember that life is not what you are given, but how you react to it.

22. CELEBRATE EACH DAY

I'm a big believer in taking time for personal reflection—for doing an assessment on the course your life has taken and its future. During these self-assessments, you have an opportunity to discard the destructive baggage of what was, take selfless pride in what you have accomplished, and be thankful for the loving people in your life. This kind of reflection brings about an appreciation for each day and makes living more enjoyable.

To know there are those who love you, respect you, and appreciate you is a primary reason to wake up each morning, and a thankful reason to rest your head on that pillow each night. To be appreciative of each day stems from not just being thankful for what is around you, but also being thankful for what is within you. The more at peace you are with who you are, the happier each day will be.

Personal peace is the result of personal honesty and taking accountability for the choices and decisions you have made. An acceptance of self and a willingness to serve others enhances the appreciation of each experience you encounter. The timeless cliché of "It could always be worse" is not something to be used as an excuse for not taking responsibility for what may have occurred, but rather an instrument to know how blessed you may be.

A NEWFOUND APPRECIATION

In 2011 I ruptured my bicep tendon, and as a result I had surgery and a cast put in place. Ironically, I was scheduled to conduct a presentation for a Wounded Warrior Symposium in Indianapolis. I acknowledged the subtle humor with my physical predicament and the venue in which I was speaking. Presenting with the cast on was challenging and a bit cumbersome because it restricted my normal animated passion while presenting. However, the wake-up call occurred when the speaker before me wheeled himself up on stage, absent of both legs and minimal use of one arm. Seeing and listening to my fellow graduate from West Point share his combat experience, I humbly realized that I was having a pretty good day.

It has been, and always will be, the greatest challenges in your life that will create the greatest understanding of who you are. Without confronting trials and tribulations, you have no way to decipher an understanding of the values you believe to be most important. It is this understanding that provides the resilience and strength to persevere.

There was a moment during his speech when my fellow alumnus shared that he contemplated suicide, but realized he had others who loved him regardless of being wheelchair bound. It was an opportunity to be stronger, set a proper example for those around him, and not use his situation as an excuse to not be giving, loving, and an honorable father and husband.

What did you wake up and whine about today? What you don't have? What you should have? What you should have done? What someone did to you four years ago? Such an attitude generates self-centeredness, encourages negativity, and initiates a mindset of entitlement. How can you appreciate each day when you are not even appreciative of yourself?

Five keys to appreciating each day are:

- Know and accept that there are those who love you, believe in you, and want you in their life. You have the ability to make a positive difference in the life of another by the example you set every day.

- Take a life break and treasure the beauty around you. A simple flower, a blue sky, a sunset, or even a changing leaf put things in perspective in regard to what a miraculous world we live in.

- Realize you have purpose and have the opportunity to live a purposeful life.

- Recognize what you do have instead of what you don't have, and experience the joy of being more selfless than self-centered.

- Live the values you believe in. It provides the framework to appreciate who you are, and therefore appreciate each day.

Make it a wonderful day!

23. MATERIALISM – TARNISHING GENUINE JOY

What does it mean to really be joyful? Does joy present itself because of outside factors, or is joy a state of being? I've often said that love, selflessness, respect, compassion, empathy, and patience are the ultimate gifts we can give to one another—that they are far more important than anything money can buy.

It is your awareness of being thoughtful and the emotional character-istics of your humanness that allows the experience of joy. A gesture of kindness, a hug shared, an ear to listen, a shoulder to lean on, a word of comfort, and a meal to nourish are all joyous moments. The giving of yourself for the betterment of another is an exercise in joyous living. The most enduring, meaningful, and memorable moments in life have nothing to do with possessions, but rather the result of the love, tutelage, and mentorship you have provided to another.

With the continued onslaught of a digital world, genuine joy is being replaced with the desire for genuine stuff. Materialism is defined as "a tendency to consider material possessions and physical comfort as more important than spiritual values." Historically, many once great societies destroyed themselves when the priority of material possessions took pre-cedence over the priority of how they conducted themselves as a people. How long have we as an American society been prioritizing things over behavior, and what will our future be?

The false joy resulting from the immediate gratification of having abundant stuff deteriorates the amazing quality of what it means to be abundantly human. An element of that amazing quality is our ability to think beyond the here and now by envisioning the potential of what could be. Is that vision for the greater good or for individual desire? For a mutually respectful heterogeneous society or a self-centered homoge-neous society? I would hope we would all work toward the greater good and celebrate the wonderment of our differences.

PEACE, LOVE, AND JOY

The opportunity to experience joy also rests with recognizing the power of peace in your life. With conflict there is mental anguish; with peace there is serenity. Joy is rarely experienced when mental anguish abounds. Joy and peace have always been celebrated as universal themes during the holiday season. But the real question is, are you living those themes and promoting them each day?

Simplicity contributes to the establishment of joy and peace in your life. Materialism creates complexity and counters simplicity because there is more stuff to be responsible for, thus adding an element of stress to contend with. In reality, an obsession with acquiring excess stuff is in many ways a substitute for not dealing with yourself and the real important personal issues that stand in the way of obtaining genuine happiness, peace, and joy.

Love is a word used consistently in regard to relationships, but what does it truly mean to love? What is your capability to love another based on? And how is that love best demonstrated? Is it through the material stuff you give? Or the selfless acts of kindness, empathy, and thoughtfulness you provide to those you share your life with?

Now, more than ever, there is a prominent need to renew our commitment to one another as a principled people, and not as principled shoppers. Be an example to others of what joy and joyous living are. It'll make you, and others, happier.

24. REFLECT ON THANKS AND GIVING

As I sat at Albany International Airport, I was dismayed that my flight was delayed due to the "Standby Horizon Indicator" instrument failing. This instrument is the primary back up to the "Main Aircraft Attitude Indicator" that displays the "Attitude" of the aircraft. Attitude is "the orientation of an aircraft or spacecraft, relative to the direction of travel." As I pondered the reason for the delay I found it interesting how "attitude" in aviation jargon is aligned with attitude in one's personal life (i.e., relative to a person's direction of travel). Apparently "attitude" is a critical component to both safe air travel and personal success. I was thankful the instrument failure occurred on the ground, not while we were in the air. It was just another reminder of how we can find things to be thankful for every day.

Of course, the current events of our world can make being thankful difficult for many. Senseless shootings, lingering wars, and economic turmoil are just a few things we as a society have witnessed and endured. With the advancement of technology increasing the speed and amount of information we are exposed to, the daily happenings of the world can become overwhelming and discouraging. That's why we all need to take a break from the disappointments of a world that seems in disarray and celebrate the simple things.

SHARE YOUR LOVE

Throughout my life, I have learned that a simple life is a happy life because there's less to be responsible for. Reflect on the amount of responsibilities you have chosen to carry and ensure those burdens are not released in destructive ways to those you care about. Then, take a deep breath and appreciate the good you have done as an individual, as a family member, and as a community member. I am thankful for the opportunity to live in a community with thoughtful, talented, and generous citizens.

Use this time not to reflect on what you have been through, but rather on those who have helped you persevere what you have been through. Who have been your mentors and role models? When was the last time you demonstrated appreciation for those who have given to you, not just material things, but also life altering and life learning insight? During the course of my own life, it was a significant challenge to allow myself to be emotionally intimate with others, resulting from losing my father at an early age. I would push away any deep level of intimacy for the fear of losing again and having to go through the anguish I had experienced as a child. Of course, that is *no excuse* for not sharing the love and appreciation for the many value lessons many have taught me, for there will come a time when I will no longer have the opportunity to share those thoughts and express my gratitude for the positive difference they made.

I recently conducted a presentation for a school district in Long Island, and the following is an email I received afterwards:

"I was in your November 3rd audience. Your message changed my life...I have now contacted my biological father, half sister and cousins that I haven't spoken with in 10 years due to fear of the unknown and what others thought of me. Your message has forever made an imprint on my soul... you spoke about not having regrets and forgiveness being like bad renters... it resonates through my mind each day and my heart as well....I am looking forward to having my family reunited soon...thank you...I hope to meet you again soon...this time with my family with me..."

Take time to show those you love how much you love them. Wake up every day knowing there is a reason why you are here. Be thankful for you and for those around you.

25. RESPECT AND VALUE LIFE

Recently I watched an October 2008 re-run of a *60 Minutes* documentary about a Spanish Bullfighter named Fracisco Rivera Ordonez and his escapades in the ring. Watching this spectacle of animal cruelty, I was genuinely disgusted by this venue of suffering and torture of life. Although I have always been aware of bull fighting and the gala of pomp and circumstance surrounding the matadors, my thoughts took me to a visceral level of anger and disgust. The accolades of courage and professionalism directed to this matador by the interviewer undermined my understanding of what those significant character traits mean.

However, the interview did reinforce my understanding of what "narcissism" means, specifically "excessive or erotic interest in oneself and one's physical appearance." Although it takes guts to get in a ring with a raging bull, what is the objective of the ensuing battle except entertainment, wealth, and fame? Why not have a few human gladiators murder one another in the ring as an encore? If NFL Quarterback Michael Vick was considered a murderous thug and imprisoned for promoting and participating in dog fighting, shouldn't these matadors be imprisoned and fined for single handedly killing over a thousand bulls over the course of their invigorating career, regardless of culture?

It is estimated there are at least 40,000 bulls killed each year in Europe and over 250,000 worldwide each year. I even read one report of an 11-year-old Franco-Mexican bullfighter who killed six young bulls during one performance. That should teach many young people about the value and dignity of life, you think? There are many other examples of such animal cruelty from the massacre of elephants, whales, dolphins, and many other species of endangered and non-endangered animals.

RESPECT FOR ALL

Why would I broach this topic? I am not an extreme environmentalist, nor am I an animal rights activist. However, while I always believe in common sense and non-extremism, I also believe in the ethical treatment of human beings and animals. Viewing this documentary caused me to sadly reflect on this travesty, and to direct thought and appreciation toward the wonderment and beauty of nature and the amazing creations that surround us. I understand there are millions of animals slaughtered for food and human consumption, but I do not know how many cattle and chickens are being slaughtered for entertainment.

As the sun blazed brightly this past week creating anticipation of an upcoming spring, I paid more attention to the little things of nature we often take for granted. The cackling of geese high in the sky returning from their southern vacation; the awakening of local birds, bugs, and critters from their wintry confinement; and the mystical lady bugs magically appearing out of nowhere are all a tribute to the miracle of nature. The warmth of a new day as the Northern Hemisphere begins to tilt forward toward the sun invigorates the soul. The expectation of flowers, colors, scents, and sounds resonate an excitement for days outdoors, walks in the park, hikes in the Adirondack High Peaks, and swims in mountain lakes.

I speak of core values as a foundation for our lives, and I have decided to add a new one: "a greater respect for life," human, animal, botanical, and even astronomical. Of course, there are many issues where the term "life" can be a platform for debate and division, but that is for a different venue. However, my heart does hope that the same level of attention, preferably a greater level, is placed on respecting human life as may be placed on an animal's life.

Five "smile creating" tips to enhance your appreciation of your surroundings are:

- Look up and observe the sun, stars, sky, etc.

- Smell a flower or bouquet.

- Listen to the sounds of chirping, barking, meowing, and squeaking.

- Wonder over the amazing details of how something as simple as a bug can be so unique.

- Experience the gentle eyes of the many animals we encounter, and just let them be.

Each day is a day to be grateful, and each day is a day to be accepting of the simple yet significant part we play in the evolution of the world.

26. RESURRECTION – A TIME TO BEGIN ANEW

Every year, people of the Christian faith celebrate the Easter Holiday, which is a time to reflect on the life, death, and resurrection of Jesus. For many who celebrate this holiday, including myself, his resurrection is an enduring reflection of the hope, love, goodness, and forgiveness that we all have the ability to exemplify.

Regardless of your faith, an understanding that each day is an opportunity to resurrect your own internal goodness is vital to a happy and fulfilling life. To forgive your past mistakes and failures, as well as those who have hurt you, is a challenging task. But doing so will have a renewing, freeing, and rewarding outcome. The meaning of the resurrection is more than just a moment in time. It is a moment in time that never dies for it continues in the spirit of all of us and all that is around us. As Martin Luther said, "Our Lord has written the promise of resurrection, not in books alone, but in every leaf of springtime."

A definition of resurrection is "the revitalization or revival of something, revive the practice, use, or memory of (something); bring new vigor to." What might you want to revitalize in your life, or bring an element of vigor? It is easy to focus on what might have been, could have been, and should have been. It is more difficult to let go of yesterday, work in the present, and plan for your future.

What are the values that structure your present and build your future? What elements of your life are you wishing to resurrect and improve upon? Your attitude, work skills, education, health, nutrition, compassion, empathy, and professionalism are all examples of areas you may wish to revisit, assess, and improve upon. To take accountability for what was, recognize what needs to improve, and live the ethical core values you believe in is a resurrection worth experiencing.

RESURRECT A POSITIVE ATTITUDE

We all have our struggles. No one is from a perfectly functional family, nor has a problem free existence. However, the ability to persevere through the dysfunctions and the problematic issues will rely on the very values that form your character, strengthen your resiliency, and solidify your self-respect. When made aware, we all have the ability to resurrect our own foundation of worth and be the example to resurrect the goodness in those around us. As Hillary Clinton stated, "It is often when night looks darkest, it is often before the fever breaks, that one senses the gathering momentum for change, when one feels that resurrection of hope in the midst of despair and apathy."

An attitude of "can do" is essential to the accomplishment of what "will be." Resurrect your inner spirit and drive to be the best you can be in all you do. Initiate resurgence in goodness, and be a positive example by the ethical behaviors that define a person of integrity. Resurrect a personal understanding that we all may be somewhat different in personality and viewpoints, but very similar in the desire for happiness and respect.

To be resurrected in spirit does not contain negativity, prejudice, judgment or self-centeredness, but rather a selfless joy in recognizing the spirit in everyone and the positive abilities that each person possesses. It may be an idealistic thought, but why not believe and hope for the best in humanity. As author Aberjhani said, "Hearts rebuilt from hope resurrect dreams killed by hate."

It is never too late to explore the best in you. A rebirth of spirit and the meaningful essence of our existence are lifelong journeys to attest the very fabric of the amazing potential of every human being, and the contribution each of us can make. Being honest with who you are and what you stand for reignites your personal spirit and the belief that you can be all you want to be and wish for. As the Resurrection is the very cornerstone that defines Christianity, resurrection of the spirit and a rebirth in the personal belief in your potential is the cornerstone to a bright future, contentment, and ultimate happiness. As Frederick W.

Robertson said, "He alone can believe in immortality who feels the resurrection in him already."

Gratitude will resurrect your spirit and be a cornerstone for developing a level of humility in your life appreciated by those around you.

SECTION FOUR

HUMILITY

"There is nothing noble in being superior to your fellow man;
true nobility is being superior to your former self."
— Ernest Hemingway

Are you better than the rest? A healthy belief in yourself is important to the accomplishment of everything you may strive for, but to negate the recognition of the value of others in your life is self-destructive. Daily, there are those in positions of influence who implode on themselves as a result of believing they are above others in regard to their own sense of self-importance. To associate with egotistical and narcissistic people is an invitation for potential personal and professional disaster. Why? They do not care about anyone other than themselves, and in many cases they destroy family, friends, and colleagues on their journey to grandiosity. The material or power gains that come from egotistical and narcissistic behavior are always at the expense of others. You will discover that the more you think of others, the happier you will tend to be and the more love you will experience in your life.

What does it mean to be humble? Humility is defined as "a modest or low view of one's own importance; humbleness." That does not mean a low view of your own capabilities and talents. That does not mean that what you do, and will do, is not important, but rather that you take the time to recognize the importance of others. Importance is "the state or fact of being of great significance or value." To believe we all have the ability and opportunity to be of great significance, or value, is the foundation for being a humble person.

The principles in this section are designed to create a greater level of awareness in the importance of others and in the example you set in demonstrating that awareness. Possessing genuine humility demonstrates an innate caring and respect toward the value of others. A humble leader, parent, or influential person will develop a loyal following, because those who follow believe they are valued.

To be truly humble is to have confidence in your own abilities and yet recognize your own inabilities. To respect those whose abilities may be your own inabilities is to acknowledge the value in others. Humility is not a weakness but strength in character, for it contains elements of respect, goodness, appreciation, selflessness, and thoughtfulness. Humility is not about how low you view your own importance, but rather how high you raise others.

27. APPRECIATING THE YOUNGSTER IN ALL OF US

When I reflect on my younger days—the days many people yearn to relive or recapture—I realize that I am happier now than those many years ago. I may have had a bit more energy, been in better physical shape, and more prone to taking risks, but the abundance and joy of living today comes from within. This is only revealed to each of us, celebrated, and understood with experience and maturity. To witness your efforts, successes, perseverance through failures, and execution of your core values come to fruition is a time for appreciation and quiet reflection. Albert Einstein said, "I live in that solitude which is painful in youth, but delicious in the years of maturity."

There is no one, no family and no life that is perfect, and the journey of your life's choices will bring joy, challenge and at times sadness. That's because the journey is not supposed to be an easy one—it's meant to be challenging and demanding, for without the struggles you cannot discover your successes.

Youth is an opportunity to discover and learn from those who came before you. What is our youth learning from us and those who came before us? I find it interesting how generation after generation tends to point fingers at the youth of the day for many of society's ills. Is it me, or were we all not part of a younger generation at one time? I find it humorous that a Baby Boomer, such as myself, could ever say with a straight face that growing up we were pure as the driven snow in all our behaviors and attitudes. Anybody remember the 60s? Many years ago, I can vividly remember my parents reflecting on my generation stating, "What is this world coming to?"

Yet, it is and has always been the younger generation that eventually replaces the present one and carries the torch. And with it has come enhanced creativity, innovation, technology, and amazing human advancements. If there are aspects of the younger generation that disturb you, what are you doing as a parent, professional, community leader, and citizen to lessen that disturbance? What are your expectations of the younger generation, and are you setting an example that would live up to your own expectations?

YOU CAN SHAPE THE FUTURE

I have served on my local school board and have coached our youth. I am currently serving on the local Congressional Service Academy Selection Committee, and I continue to be a parent. In all those capacities, I have witnessed the skills and talents our youth possess and the accomplishments that many have achieved. I realize that it is not the time to disparage our youth, but to motivate, inspire, and encourage our young people to work hard and achieve their dreams. We must provide them the insight to live up to their potential.

If we want our children to be ethical, accountable, mannerly, respectful, and have a strong work ethic, we as the adults must set the example. Why would a child believe in the importance of being accountable when there are adults who blame everything around them for the failures in their life? Why would a child believe in the importance of being ethical and honorable when there are adults who are dishonest and dishonorable? Why would a child believe in what intrinsically brings happiness when society is focused on materialism, consumption, an acceptance of disrespect, and a lack of civility?

Throughout my years of speaking, which includes young audiences, I have always found our youth yearning for structure, discipline, and those who have the character to stand up for what they feel is right. There is no respect generated by the young toward an elder if the elder lacks moral fortitude and integrity, and is inconsistent in their beliefs and behaviors.

Our youth want to learn. They want strong examples and they desire to be better than those from generations past. If we as adults, parents, and community leaders do not take the high road, why would we expect our youth to be any different? Let us all display a belief in the goodness and potential of our youth, not through artificial praise and giving them trophies for showing up to practice, but rather by providing them the time, energy, and positive examples they need. It's up to each of us to be a role model for them to have a bright and fulfilling future. As Ralph Waldo Emerson said, "The search after the great men is the dream of youth, and the most serious occupation of manhood."

28. CLASS WARFARE - A DANGER TO COMPARE

The current emphasis on class warfare by mainstream media and political circles is creating social dissension, and is dividing rather than uniting this nation. Historically, most revolutions have started as a result of the polarizing differences between those who have more and those who have less. There is no doubt differences exist and are becoming more extensive. We all have a responsibility as citizens to create an environment of equality and fairness.

I am not sharing these thoughts to debate a strategy on how to bring peace among the classes, but rather to encourage you to not allow the battle to determine your sense of self-worth. There will always be those who have more stuff, but that is not an excuse to believe that those who have less are less of a person or that those who have more are more of a person. Humility plays a vital role in decreasing the temptation to compare. The essence of humility never includes the element of comparison, but rather promotes a behavior of compassion.

Each day we are inundated with what others have versus what we ourselves have. Comparing the value of one another based on things rather than substance of character is emotionally self-destructive. Greed always creates a greater potential for destructive and unethical behavior. Frequently we witness the consequences of greed and the debilitating impact it has on the ethical and moral foundation of all society. But realize that the individuals in your life who made a positive and enduring impact were never about what they owned. It was always the content of their character and the values they espoused that made them special. There will always be unfairness and inequality, but two wrongs do not make a right.

Leaders today must take logical, uniting, and common sense actions to balance class differences, bring greater harmony among the classes, and level the playing field. To blame and create dissension only manifests distrust, thereby initiating anger and violence. Individually, to become discouraged and angry over others' possessions is unhealthy in regard to your own sense of self-respect. Your importance as a person is not relative to what you have, but rather who you are. I have always believed we should help those who are in need, and as a society we have an obligation to assist those who are less fortunate. It is when there is a loss of common cause and concern for one another that a society begins to fracture.

WHAT VALUES DO YOU REFLECT?

Realize that it is more important to live a life that is a reflection of the values you believe in than your ability to purchase another bargain. There is no doubt that it can be frustrating and dispiriting to see the lifestyles of those who have more, but to equate that to the value and self-respect you have for yourself is a choice you make. In addition, when you use comparison of class as an excuse for not taking owner-ship for your personal and professional behavior, the fight for fairness is tarnished and less credible.

It would be encouraging to witness political leaders emphasize more of what we have in common as a people rather than our differences. It does not negate the necessity to confront and address the social and economic issues at hand, but to manipulate the masses by exploiting their differences only makes the challenge for fairness and equality more difficult. Dr. Martin Luther King, Jr. stated, "The ultimate measure of a man is not where he stands in moments of comfort, but where he stands at times of challenge and controversy." It will be your strength to act on the core values you believe in that will allow you to stand in those moments. Leadership that creates mutual respect and trust is a result of skills and traits that unify not divide. As the Latin writer of maxims, Publius Syrus, noted, "The greater a man is in power above others, the more he ought to excel them in virtue. None ought to govern who is not better than the governed."

Personal honesty is more important than personal possessions. How we treat one another, and the greater example of selflessness and hu-mility we demonstrate, will ultimately determine the level of difference between us as a people. We are fortunate to have the freedom to work for the causes we believe in, and therefore a responsibility to continue to strive toward fairness and equality for all.

29. REGRETS – TIME TO TAKE OUT THE TRASH

If there is one area of your emotional thought process that stifles personal and professional development beyond all others, it is to be continually regretful for the perceived and actual mistakes you have made. You cannot change the past, nor is it beneficial to use regrets as excuses for not being the person you can be today. Mistakes are made, dysfunctions are created, and insecurities generated; but to be consumed by what wasn't depletes the very essence of what could be. To acknowledge what you may be regretful for is to also recognize the potential lessons learned from those mistakes made.

Sincere and genuine regret is accepting and taking accountability for behaviors that most likely violated a fundamental core value you believe in. For example, if a core value of yours is loyalty and you breech that loyalty in a relationship or business venture, and the outcome is distrust and failure, then say hello to the makings of a regret. If a core value of yours is integrity and you violate the very essence of standing your ground honorably and treating others with dignity and respect, regret will be the outcome.

Regret is defined as "a feeling of sadness, repentance, or disappointment over something that has happened or been done." How often do we tend to beat ourselves up over the mistakes we have made instead of putting our efforts toward being a better person, parent, or professional today? The choice to use yesterday's failures as today's excuses is emotionally destructive. Stop hoping for a better past! Constant regret does nothing to neither develop nor substantiate a strong character or contribute to a legacy that is positive and enduring. As novelist and poet C. S. Lewis said, "Has this world been so kind to you that you should leave with regret? There are better things ahead than any we leave behind."

What do you want to leave behind? Or in other words, what would you like to be remembered for? To focus on regrets will never contribute to a positive memory of you from those who love you. Regret is the thief that steals a strong character and a solid sense of self-respect.

SAY "GOOD RIDDANCE" TO REGRETS

Following the core values you believe in and acting on those values provides you the strength to conquer regret and move forward with the life you know you should lead. Regardless of what others may harbor from the mistakes or decisions you have made, it is your conscious choice to release the burdens of negativity and take control of your life for the betterment of those around you that will lead to personal fulfillment. When your heart is true to the goodness you believe in and your soul is on a path of purpose, then what was done or what others may think of you now is irrelevant to the honorable path you have chosen. As Henry David Thoreau stated, "Never look back unless you are planning to go that way."

To go back is to disavow and devalue your future, and you are too valuable a person to go down that path. You must recognize that there are those who love you, respect you, and look up to you; and you owe it to those who see you in that light to set an example of optimism, purpose, servitude, and mentorship.

Regrets can educate us in regard to what we wished to have done better, and that is the one beauty of regret. To take accountability for what you regret is a catalyst to be better than what you were and to learn from the mistakes you made. Renewing, reflecting, and reinforcing the core values that form your character are the steps to building a foundation of no regrets. It is the process of putting into practice again and again the values that form that character that will diminish the regrets you may have from yesterday, and lead to a positive and lasting legacy in the future. As Alexander Graham Bell said, "When one door closes, another opens; but we often look so long and so regretfully upon the closed door that we do not see the one which has opened for us." Say hello to making an effort to forego what wasn't and living a life of what can be.

30. ACTIVATE YOUR BUCKET LIST TODAY

Life is too short to worry about all the things that are wrong with it. Rather, it's more important to cherish all the things that are wonderful about life. I realize that the quality of my physical life 20 years from now will be substantially less than it is today. There is also a good chance every day might be a new day depending on my future mental well-being. Some in my life have already made that call for the latter.

There is no doubt you are young at heart, as am I, and we would not have it any other way. However, the days still pass, so you have to make the best of them. Although your mind may say "yes," your body may occasionally provide a wake-up call that you're not as young as you think. Passion for life and the people you love are the inspiration for a youthful heart, a gracious spirit, and a willing body. Though you cannot know what tomorrow may bring, a positive, humble, and selfless attitude today will make every moment a bit more joyful.

The theme of the movie *The Bucket List* (2007) is a list of things the two main characters, played by Jack Nicholson and Morgan Freeman, wish to do before they "kick the bucket" (i.e., die, as both of them are terminally ill). I encourage you to create, activate, and participate in your bucket list today. You are never too young to hope and plan for what you desire.

What are your dreams, aspirations, and heartfelt wishes in life? That once-in-a-lifetime trip, a completed physical challenge, a degree, owning your own business, a passion to cook, a desire to paint (or sing or dance), and a relationship to fulfill are all examples of what could be in your bucket. No regrets, no excuses, and you must believe no one will prevent you from checking off that list. It is a core belief in you and what you stand for and believe in that will propel you to fulfill those desires.

AN EMPTY BUCKET FOR A HAPPY LIFE
You may find yourself overwhelmed with the amount on your list. Take the time to prioritize what you wish for most. Subsequently, evaluate it, budget it, plan it, and make a commitment to make it happen.

What is there to lose but time…and that's the point. As in any endeavor, the road to accomplishment is never easy, and checking off your bucket list items is no different. The life skills of self-discipline, resiliency, determination, and perseverance are as needed to empty the bucket as they are to overcome the trials and tribulations you face every day. Would it not be more enjoyable and fulfilling to focus your energy on emptying the bucket? As Ralph Waldo Emerson quoted, "Life is a journey not a destination." And Aristotle so eloquently stated, "Happiness is the meaning of the purpose of life, the whole aim and end of human existence." What are you waiting for?

Granted, emptying the entire bucket may be unrealistic, but making a commitment to enjoy the journey is essential for long-term happiness. The absence of a bucket list in your life is the first step to waking up with less purpose and acquiring a pessimistic view of your future. Without something to look forward to, you will emotionally and physically deteriorate. Living life to the fullest is not about allowing life to control you, but rather assimilating the values you believe in and the desires you wish for within the sphere of living.

Three gifts to being human are having the ability to smile, laugh, and cry. How wonderful to be complete in the expression of what it means to be alive. Discard your frailties, forgive your mistakes, forgive others who have harmed you, love those who love you, and appreciate the little things that bring happiness to your life. A full bucket has the potential to provide nourishment for many. Strive to empty the bucket while bringing happiness to yourself and those around you. Enjoy the pour.

31. A FATHER'S DAY RESPONSIBILITY

As I was sitting on a flight to Vancouver, BC to share my No Excuse! message with an organization recently, it occurred to me that it was once again the anniversary of my father's death from a heart attack, June 7, 1968, at the age of 49. As mentioned previously, I was eleven years old at the time and I can still vividly remember the day: I was sitting in my sixth grade class when I heard an ambulance siren blaring outside. Intuitively I knew my father was in that ambulance. Later that day my uncle met me at the bus stop and told me the news. When I got home, I saw the sorrow in the familiar faces of those around me. I remember my mother's shock, my sister's tears, and my uncle's effort to keep some semblance of order in the midst of emotional chaos.

In the days that followed, relatives I had not seen in years, and friends, with their outpouring of sympathy just heightened the impact of the event. Seemingly numb at the funeral and finally crying as the casket was being lowered into the ground, I knew there would be difficult days ahead. I wondered what tomorrow would bring without a paternal influence. So many questions raced through my mind: "How will I know how to be a good father, a loving husband, and a man of character myself? Who will teach and mentor me? How will I have the courage to be emotionally intimate again with those I love when it hurt so much to lose the father I loved? Why did this have to happen and what do I do from here?"

All of these questions and more could have easily become excuses to ruin my life. Instead, the questions became a subconscious motivation to find the answers and eventually gain a thorough understanding that excuses are the antithesis of personal accountability. That may appear to be common knowledge and it should be, but how many put into practice that understanding?

Understanding and projecting a belief is easy; implementing that belief is the ultimate test of individual character. I believe what happens to you happens *for* you, and it is an outlook on life that has served me well over the years. Those questions directed me to the path I am on, for you teach best in life what you want to learn the most. My journey of growing as a man continues and with it comes a responsibility to those around me, especially those I love.

WHAT FATHERHOOD REALLY MEANS

Fathers of good character are needed now more than ever. Our children deserve strong male role models, not simply based on muscle, brawn, and title, but on strength of character, humility, and demonstrated positive core values. Over the many years I have been far from perfect in my fathering skills, but I am still a dad and I continue to strive to be a better one every day. Your children will not care about what you had, only who you were and the example you set. My children have loved me unconditionally through the many ups and downs of my own journey and I will be forever grateful for their love, empathy, and support. It is fascinating to reflect on how many times our own children teach us how to be better parents.

In the United States, every June we celebrate Father's Day to remember and appreciate the fathers in our lives. But it should also be a day for each father to reflect on the example they set each day. I hope the fathers you know set an example of care, love, strength, and mentorship, to name a few.

What does it mean to be a dad? From my personal perspective, I believe it means:

- A father's emotional presence for their children is as important as their physical presence.

- Asking questions is more effective than always dictating.

- It's important to reflect and listen before reacting.

- Be an example of action not just words, and a teacher not just a protector.

- Understand that anger destroys communication, while emotional patience is key to creating harmony.

- Accept the uniqueness in your children rather than always expecting them to be like you. This demonstrates respect for, and humility toward, who they are, and will generate an emotional bond that will last forever.

As Abraham Lincoln stated, "I don't know who my grandfather was; I am much more concerned to know what his grandson will be."

32. A COMMITMENT OF LOVE

On March 14, 1981, I exchanged marriage vows with a beautiful woman named Noni. We made a commitment to honor, love, and cherish one another till death do us part. Reflecting on our 30+ years of marriage, I am humbled by my wife's dedication to her family, her moral fortitude, and her lifelong support of our journey together. Actually, I should submit her application for sainthood for having the steadfast loyalty to still be with me. I can honestly state that if it were not for her internal strength of character I would not be the man, father, and husband I am today. This is a tribute to all couples that believe there is strength in togetherness and share a mutual belief in the values that make a positive difference in the lives of those around them.

Through the peaks and valleys of any relationship it is, and will be, a couple's common core values that create the resiliency to persevere through the doubtful and difficult times. I have learned over these many years (or maybe I should say "have been trained") that it is also a couple's display of mutual respect that illustrates an appreciation for one another.

Personal honesty is another key to any relationship's survival. To be honest with yourself eliminates the potential to blame your partner for your potential discontent, self-doubt, and lack of self-respect. When you take advantage of those you love and point to them as an excuse for your own insecurities, it destroys the very fabric of mutual respect, humility, trust, and lasting commitment. Disappointment with yourself is not the fault of those you love or those who love you. Using your relationship or your family as rationale for not taking ownership for your behaviors and decisions is self-destructive.

Commitment is defined as "dedication; application, a pledge or undertaking." I am sure you would agree that marriage is quite an undertaking. However, as challenging as it might be, the rewards of healthy companionship, raising a loving family, and building a life together encompasses the human experience that provides added purpose and meaning to living each day.

In celebration of this auspicious moment I thought I would share some selected insights from others in regard to their thoughts on marriage.

"Men marry women with the hope they will never change. Women marry men with the hope they will change. Invariably they are both disappointed." –Albert Einstein.

"Do you know what it means to come home at night to a woman who'll give you a little love, a little affection, a little tenderness? It means you're in the wrong house, that's what it means." –George Burns.

"In my house I'm the boss; my wife is just the decision maker." –Woody Allen.

"By all means marry; if you get a good wife, you'll be happy. If you get a bad one, you'll become a philosopher." –Socrates.

"I love being married. It's so great to find that one special person you want to annoy the rest of your life." –Rita Rudner.

"Newlyweds become oldyweds, and oldyweds are the reasons that families work." –Author Unknown.

"Never go to bed mad. Stay up and fight." –Phyllis Diller.

"Don't marry the person you think you can live with; marry the individual you think you can't live without." –James C. Dobson.

"Come, let's be a comfortable couple and take care of each other! How glad we shall be, that we have somebody we are fond of always, to talk to and sit with." –Charles Dickens.

"Some people ask the secret to our long marriage. We take time to go to a restaurant two times a week. A little candlelight, dinner, soft music, and dancing. She goes Tuesdays; I go Fridays." –Henny Youngman.

"What a happy and holy fashion it is that those who love one another should rest on the same pillow." –Nathaniel Hawthorne.

As the years have passed I have grown to love my wife more each day. It has been a trip with twists and turns along the way, as well as moments of wondering what tomorrow may bring. Although not always a vacation, the adventure has brought with it a love and a friendship that will never end. I am thankful to have married up.

33. PRIDE AND SIGNIFICANCE – YOU REALLY DO MATTER

Have you ever felt insignificant or asked yourself, "Does anything I do really matter in relation to the world around me?" Perhaps you've wondered, "I drive to work each day. I do my job. I try to make a difference. Am I doing the right thing? Do those around me appreciate me? Does anyone really care? In the scheme of time, space, and living each day, do I make a positive impact, and is it really meaningful in the long run?"

Are these questions depressing? You bet! This type of thought process and attitude is the antithesis of possessing pride. Yet, pride is a word that tends to be frowned upon. Why? The saying, "pride goes (or comes) before a fall" is a proverb that means if you are too conceited or self-important, something will happen to make you look foolish. Although at times this may indeed happen, pride is not something to shy away from. It is important to be proud of who you are and what you stand for and believe in.

When pride is genuine, selfless, and honest, the feeling and modest display of such pride is healthy and important in validating for yourself that who you are and what you do is significant. Pride is defined as "a feeling or deep pleasure or satisfaction derived from one's own achievements, the achievements of those with whom one is closely associated with, or from qualities or possessions that are widely admired, the consciousness of one's own dignity."

Dignity? Dignity is defined as "the state or quality of being worthy of honor or respect." Who would not want to possess that state or quality? Personally, if I have achieved in an ethical and upstanding manner, and generate a degree of honor and respect within myself and from others, I would certainly be proud of that accomplishment. It does not mean you take an attitude of self-importance over humility, but if you are not proud in what you have achieved then why did you strive for anything to begin with? Pride becomes harmful when it transitions into the behaviors of conceit, vanity, arrogance, and egotism.

DISPLAY SELFLESS PRIDE

Pride should also be modest, not boastful. There is no doubt that actions speak louder than words, and it is recognizing and acting upon that thought that eliminates the potential to be boastful. However, it is also interesting to observe that the more insecure someone is with him or herself, the more likely that person is to accuse another of being overly proud. When another succeeds it can be threatening to those who doubt their own abilities. It is your own recognition of how you display your pride that will determine how valid another's negative assessment of your behavior may be. When your pride is attached to humility and selflessness there is no need for concern about how others perceive it. It becomes more about them than their negative perception of you.

As I write this, I am on a plane to L.A., and at this moment our cat of almost 21 years, Cleo, is being euthanized. She had been failing for days and we made the difficult decision to end her suffering. I know my wife and son are with her, holding, loving, and comforting her as the injection takes effect. As I said my goodbyes this morning before I left for the airport, a characteristic that came to mind of my beloved feline was pride. She always displayed pride in herself, her family, her longevity, and doing things her way. As she lay dying this morning, she was still purring as I stroked her head, as soft and furry as it had always been. I believe she was proud of the joy, love, and memorable times she had provided to our family over all these years.

Selfless pride is a characteristic of having done more for others than yourself. It is a characteristic of personal confidence that others admire and follow, for it is genuine, sincere, and never boastful. Take a moment to appreciate yourself and what you have accomplished in your life. Be proud of the times where you made a positive difference in the life of another. As Ralph Waldo Emerson so eloquently stated, "To know just one life has breathed easier because you have lived, this is to have succeeded." You can take pride in that.

34. A TRIBUTE TO A MOTHER'S LOVE

In April 2013 as I sat by my mother's bedside as she prepared to go to her heavenly Father, I reflected on how deep a love can be between a mother and son. She was there when I took my first breath, and it was only fair that I be there for her last. Although so terribly sad, it was also joyful and humbling to reminisce on her life, family, friends, and happy memories.

Dorothy Rifenbary was a woman of principle and conviction, and she had a sense of humor that was with her to the end. As I shared with her that she would be forever healthy where she was going, she responded, "Which way am I going—up or down?" Of course, laughter was shared as I held her hand and assured her that it was most likely up.

She had a passion for life that included her love of family, service to her community, and enjoying as many rounds of golf as possible. And her day wasn't complete without a little nip of her Smirnoff martini. Mom was 44 years young when her husband, my father, passed away from cardiac arrest. From that moment, she was determined to not permit the loss of a husband and father to be used an excuse not to persevere. She dedicated her life to exemplify strength of personal character and a devotion to her children. Mom was committed to instilling manners in her children and had an expectation of respectfulness from all she encountered. Her enthusiastic spirit and infectious zest for life will be remembered and treasured beyond her mortal life.

As the priest administered "last rites" with family at her side, she participated with a faithfulness of optimism and peace that was spiritually comforting to herself and all who were present. The strength of a family's love conquers all opposition to the goodness of humanity. If you consider intestinal fortitude to be a core value, then my mother was the queen of that personal characteristic.

What values do you admire of those you love? Have you ever shared with them your appreciation for those values they exemplify? Every day is a day to be giving, to be thoughtful of others, and to be thankful for the blessings you have. Mom lived a full life with joy and sadness, success and defeat, assuredness and self-doubt, but she never gave up on her quest to make a positive difference in others and her community.

As I reflect on my childhood, I remember my mother supporting me in every endeavor, yet with a strictness of ensuring I was respectful of others and lived up to what she felt to be the standard of our family. Although I did not always comply with her expectations by my actions, her expectations and what she felt I could achieve was always part of my mindset. As Mark Twain stated, "My mother had a great deal of trouble with me, but I think she enjoyed it." It was that consistency of expectation that was a catalyst for me in striving to be the best husband, father, professional, and person I could be.

Our final days together were a time of reflection, apologies, forgiveness, smiles, tears, laughter, understanding, respect, and most important, mutual love. During the course of our relationship there were times the past would surface and result in emotional impatience, but the love between mother and son was always present. Our love was strong and genuine enough to endure all that we had experienced together. To say that her children and grandchildren respect her would be an understatement, and her love will forever be part of each of us.

As a son, I could not have asked for a better role model in regard to experiencing the strength and endurance of a woman's determination. True grit was truly Dorothy.

Mom, I will always treasure my memories of your beautiful maternal spirit. Thank you for giving me life and the opportunity to experience what it means to genuinely live. Please say hello to Dad for me. I know the both of you are already enjoying a round of golf and are making up for the many years of love that was lost so long ago. I will forever love you.

SECTION FIVE

SELF-DISCIPLINE

"It is for us to pray not for tasks equal to our powers,
but for powers equal to our tasks, to go forward with a
great desire forever beating at the door of our hearts as
we travel toward our distant goal."
– Helen Keller

Do you have the self-discipline to reach your next level of achievement? What amount of self-discipline will you need to accomplish your desires and aspirations? With self-discipline there is consistency in action. With self-discipline there is an adherence to the core values that structure what you stand for and believe in. As a result, there are parameters of behavior to hold yourself and others accountable.

Quite simply, having self-discipline is having the resiliency, based on a solid foundation of core values, to sustain your ability to persevere to the accomplishment of your goals. In any endeavor it is one of the most important characteristics of a successful person. Do you have the self-discipline to eat well, exercise, be fiscally responsible, be patient, maintain your emotions, control your addictions or obsessions, and be consistent in exemplifying the values you believe in?

Having self-discipline is the result of having a solid foundation of self-respect that stems from a strong foundation of core values in your life. Self-discipline is defined as "the ability to control one's feelings and overcome one's weaknesses; the ability to pursue what one thinks is right despite temptations to abandon it." Temptations are a catalyst for distraction and a detriment to maintaining self-discipline. Additionally, when a temptation is executed it transcends into an excuse for failure. When what you are tempted toward compromises the core values you believe in, your need for self-discipline is the greatest.

The principles in this section are designed to provide you with the foundation and skills to maintain a consistent level of self-discipline in all your endeavors. It is making your mind up to stay on track and continue down a path toward success no matter the challenges. There may be failures along the way, but the journey will educate you and you will be stronger for it. To overcome the distractions and temptations in your life will consistently build the strength of your character and generate respect from others.

Life is not meant to be easy. It is the testing of your self-discipline, and an understanding that what is desired needs to be earned, that builds strength of character, self-respect, and determination. Without self-discipline, you are vulnerable to the temptations and distractions of the outside, rather than creating your character from the inside.

35. TURN YOUR VULNERABILITIES INTO POSSIBILITIES

How vulnerable are you to the negative influences and the power of your own weaknesses? For example...

- Does your lack of patience make you vulnerable to anger?

- Does your lack of discipline make you vulnerable to excess?

- Does your lack of personal accountability make you vulnerable to blaming those around you for your failures?

- Does your lack of integrity make you vulnerable to the self-centered temptations of life?

- Does your lack of an understanding of what your core values are make you vulnerable to indecisiveness, self-doubt, and lacking self-respect?

- Do your insecurities make you vulnerable to being emotionally hurt?

Vulnerable is defined as "capable of, or susceptible to, being wounded or hurt, as by a weapon, a vulnerable part of the body; open to moral attack, criticism, temptation, etc."

To be vulnerable is a normal human emotion and experience. It is life's flashing warning sign notifying you of potential emotional and physical harm. However, it is also a positive sign, indicating an opportunity for you to become a stronger and better person. Your vulnerabilities are potential possibilities for greater success, happiness, and fulfillment. They make you aware of what you need to improve upon, both personally and professionally.

For example, if you are vulnerable to procrastination, it will have a detrimental impact on your ability to be self-disciplined, resulting in the inability to be as efficient and thorough with work projects you are assigned. If you are vulnerable to criticism, it will have a negative impact on your ability to be decisive, resulting in a greater lack of self-respect. Are either of those vulnerabilities excuses, or are they opportunities to overcome those weaknesses and improve the quality of your life? There are reasons in life for mistakes and failures, and they happen to all of us; however, an excuse is the consistent repetition of reasons used to justify and rationalize debilitating behavior. There are reasons for despair, anger, and disappointment, but an excuse ensures the sustainment of those reasons.

BANISH YOUR VULNERABILITIES

Can excuses be an extension of your vulnerabilities? Absolutely! If what you are vulnerable to is self-destructive, it is your decision to either make a change or decide to use it as an excuse to not live up to your potential. Overcoming your vulnerabilities spearheads achievement to further success and greater happiness, for it demonstrates strength and courage to become a better you. What steps can you take to conquer your own vulnerabilities?

- Be accountable. Begin by admitting you have vulnerabilities. Take accountability for them and have the humility to be accepting that they exist. "Pride goeth before the fall," for arrogant pride destroys character and a sense of self.

- Assess yourself. Determine which vulnerabilities are the most destructive. What has created the most stress, emotional turmoil, and indecision in your life? For example, if you are vulnerable to the pain of loss and you react defensively rather than compassionately, which behavior would you choose for an emotionally healthier you? Assessing which vulnerabilities are most harmful prioritizes which vulnerabilities to address first.

- Take action. Action is the third element, and if not implemented, accountability and assessment are irrelevant, for now avoidance has taken control. Returning to the previous example, if you do become defensive around the pain of loss, what actions are you taking to address that behavior, and what can you do to become more compassionate in the process? Action taken is never easy and in many cases it is uncomfortable, but to avoid it only enables the destructive behavior. It takes courage to change and strength of character to go the distance. Adherence to your core values provides the strength to overcome your weaknesses.

- Analyze yourself. Analysis is the fourth step to evaluate your progress in lessening the destructive powers of being vulnerable. If the proper action is taken, the analysis will be a positive one and a healthy step forward to becoming less vulnerable. Now is not the time to be defeated by what you can't do, but rather to be the champion in believing what you can become. To be a better parent, professional, spouse, and individual is never finite, but a continual process in the development of your character and the legacy of what you stood for and believed in.

View your vulnerabilities as opportunities, not liabilities. Your reward will be greater self-confidence and self-respect; self-discipline is the key.

36. RESOLUTIONS – A YEAR ROUND RESPONSIBILITY

How many New Year's resolutions come and go, only to be thought of again as the end of the year approaches? Resolutions are nice to have; acting on them is rarely easy to do. To have a resolution is a commitment to change a behavior, so it's no wonder they fade into the shadows of spring. To be resolute is the core value that provides the foundation for a successful resolution.

Resolute is defined as "firmly resolved or determined, set in purpose or opinion, characterized by firmness and determination, as the temper, spirit, actions, etc." As Abraham Lincoln said, "Always bear in mind that your own resolution is more important than any other." To be resolute takes strength of character and courage—the courage to change, to take risks, to think outside the box, to get out of your comfort zone, and most important, to understand that a successful resolution will likely have a positive impact on those around you.

A physically and emotionally healthier you is a gift to those you parent, influence, and love. Considering others into the equation of a successful resolution is the key to maintaining the motivation to complete what you set out to do. To stop smoking, eat healthy, drink less alcohol, stay in shape, and be an ethical person should be as much for your children, grandchildren, and those you love, as for yourself. To take care of yourself is not being self-centered when the benefit to your commitment is for those you love and cherish. If you do not care about yourself why would you expect others to care about you?

RESOLVE TO DITCH THE EXCUSES

What impedes a successful resolution? Excuses! You know the ones: "I don't have enough time." "I don't have the energy." "My issues aren't that bad." "Others don't really care." "I'm from a dysfunctional family." "There is always next year." "I'm really not that fat." "It can't happen to me." "It's not my fault." These are all examples of the sickness of excuses. It is always easier to resort to how it has always been, rather than to work toward what could be a better you. Doing the same thing, and expecting a different outcome, is insanity.

Denial is the stimulus for generating excuses and for the development of a lack of personal accountability. Denial in psychological terms is defined as "an unconscious defense mechanism used to reduce anxiety by denying thoughts, feeling, or facts that are consciously intolerable." How personally dishonest is denial? It is a lie directed to yourself. In simple terms, denial is a cop-out for not taking ownership for your life. As Benjamin Franklin stated, "How few there are who have the courage enough to own their faults, or resolution enough to mend them."

What is the difference between a resolution and a goal? A resolution is your intent to accomplish a goal. Without the proper execution of your intent, your goal cannot be achieved. Firm resolve is the backbone for your effort, and the accomplishment of that goal is your reward. In addition, without the element of self-discipline included in your resolve, there is minimal chance of accomplishing your goals. Change is challenging yet invigorating when you realize what you set out to do can actually come to fruition. Taking things one day at a time, having a commitment to do something each day directed toward that goal, and keeping your eye on the prize are the three pillars to keep you strong and resolute.

Another key factor in achieving that goal is your attitude. Are you optimistic about your future, or are you in the doldrums because of your negativity and despair? If pessimism is the norm, failure will be the outcome. Surrounding yourself with optimistic and successful people can break the cycle of negativity. Find those who inspire and achieve, not depress and complain. Find those who have principled values, not unprincipled behaviors.

Here's a resolution I would like everyone to consider: A social and communal resolution of commitment to unify our citizenry around mutual respect, moral decency, common sense, and integrity by the example we set each day. To realize there are those who believe in us is the reason we should believe in one another. Quitting is not an option, so make your resolutions become a reality. As the American naturalist and essayist John Burroughs simply said, "One resolution I have made, and try always to keep, is this: to rise above the little things."

37. DISCONNECT FROM TECHNOLOGY

Reflecting on a recent vacation on the beautiful Caribbean island of St. Lucia, one of the highlights was my decision not to participate in any technology. No smart phone, no iPad, and no computer. Instead, I focused on the people, culture, and nature surrounding me. As a result, I thoroughly enjoyed my time away from the normal hustle and bustle of life. During the trip, I actually took time to read a recent *National Geographic*—something I had not done in years. I had forgotten what an enlightening and educational magazine it is. Yes, I actually read the articles, and not just viewed the pictures.

My suggestion for you is to take a vacation from the world of technology at your first opportunity. Instead of punching a keypad, take a hike, exercise, read, or engage in an activity you enjoy without the use of technology. Doing so allows you to take a step back, take a deep breath, and potentially allow a moment of peaceful reflection and perspective.

The increasing speed and momentum of how we are living is stealing much of the joy and fulfillment of what it means to live as a human being. Granted, we are all dependent on varying forms of technology for the life we wish to have, but it is also technology that has realigned what is perceived to be important for a healthy lifestyle. The technology to create a life-like video game is amazing, but is sitting in front of the television or computer for hours on end contributing to a healthy life? There is no doubt that certain technology has contributed significantly to the availability of a sedentary lifestyle. The substantial increase in childhood obesity is one obvious result.

TAKE CONTROL

Is technology controlling you? Here are a few questions to consider:

- Could you make it through the day without texting someone?

- Would you know what to do with yourself if you could not check your email?

- Would you be able to keep your head up for more than a couple of minutes without being tempted to look down at your smart phone?

- Could you get through a day without logging into Facebook or Twitter?

- Are you feeling anxious just by honestly answering these questions?

- Are you really that important, and are you really that needed, that you cannot disconnect from technology for a moment?

For some, it might be frightening to even imagine how they would occupy their time without a technological device close at hand. They might actually have to entertain themselves, with their own thoughts, creativity, speech, intellect, and physical abilities.

The intentional consumption of time with technology can create a degree of neglect of the very core values that develop a well-rounded and character-based individual. Accountability, integrity, personal honesty, forgiveness, self-respect, kindness, resiliency, and perseverance are just a sampling of core values that technology has little to do with developing. Technology certainly provides greater access to knowledge, but at the end of the day it will still be the content of your character and the values you believe in that will determine your level of happiness and contentment. With everything in life comes the necessity to make responsible choices. How you use technology to your benefit or detriment is a choice.

Anything taken to an extreme is harmful, and monitoring the balance of technology in your life with how you actually live is critical for your emotional and physical well-being. There have been times when I've looked up from my computer, saw the clock, and then asked myself, "Where did the day go?"

How much time is spent during the course of the day doing technological gibberish? Instead of tweeting and telling your followers you are having a cup of coffee, how about putting that energy into something relevant and that has the potential to make a difference in yourself, others, and the community. The greatest joys in my life have had little to do with technology, and yet my greatest frustrations always have. I have always found that the simpler my life is, the happier I tend to be, because the less I have to be responsible for. As John F. Kennedy stated, "Man is still the most extraordinary computer of all." Have the self-discipline and make the time to enjoy a technology free day soon.

38. LEADERSHIP IN A.C.T.I.O.N.

What attributes are needed to be an effective leader? There are many you could list, but there are several that, when working together, create a formula for success both personally and professionally. With the increasing uncertainty in regard to our nation's economic, social, and political future, it will be ethical, principled, and common sense leadership that will save the day. In any venue where leadership is needed, finger pointing, personal agendas, dishonesty, egotism, narcissism, greed, bias, and a reluctance to change will only foster failure. Setting an example to those around you first requires an understanding of what that example should be.

When was the last time you took the opportunity to ask your children, "What are some characteristics of leadership you believe to be important?" Their responses may surprise and inspire you. We are all leaders in our own right. There are those who love you, respect you, and look up to you; you owe it to those who see you in that light to set the proper example in all you do.

So what is the formula? It is ACTION! Accountability, Courage, Trust, Integrity, Objectivity, Novelty. It will provide you a foundation of resilience, perseverance, and a value-based blueprint for success. Self-discipline is the key to taking ACTION.

CREATE YOUR ACTION PLAN

Accountability is the recognition that your life and your decisions are your responsibility. The blame game is the true number one reality show in America. Every day we witness via the media the antics of excuse making by people in positions of leadership. What message does that send to our youth? That it is okay to blame race, creed, color, parents, where we grew up, what we didn't do, what we should have done, or what someone did to us 10 years ago as justification to miserable today? We all have our issues, but life is not what you are given; it's how you react to it.

Courage is the ability to stand up for your convictions and beliefs despite danger or disapproval. Of course, those convictions and beliefs should be in the best interest of those around you and for the betterment of society in general. The establishment of principled core values provides the back-drop for courageous behavior. Core values are your suit of armor in the face of danger. The stronger the values, the less penetrable the armor will be.

Trust is the glue of every relationship in life. When trust is broken the relationship is never the same. Trust stimulates communication, and effective communication is the catalyst for efficient progress in any endeavor. In any organization or family, the flow of communication is the indicator for the level of trust that exists within that structure. We do not communicate with those we do not trust.

Integrity is consistency in behavior, and consistency in behavior is based on the core values you believe in. No one respects a leader who is indecisive and inconsistent. Consistency in behavior displays integrity, enhances the ability to be courageous, and reinforces accountability—all of which leads to trust. The definition of integrity also includes having strong moral principles and being honest. Disregard these components of integrity and you have no credibility.

Objectivity is a critical trait for proper and effective decision making. Objectivity is defined as "(of a person or their judgment) not influenced by personal feelings or opinions in considering and representing facts." That is the antithesis to what we see in much of the political decision-making. Synonyms of objectivity include impartiality, absence of bias, lack of prejudice, fairness, open-mindedness, and neutrality to name a few. That is a characteristic we all should strive for.

Novelty in leadership is what separates common leaders from remark-able leaders. To be able to be different, new, original, and unusual is what inspires followers to want change and be better than before. Novelty has created the inventions and businesses that have changed the world.

If you are accountable for your actions, have the courage to take a stand, inspire trust by communicating honestly, display integrity by being consis-tent, be objective and display respect for all, and be novel in your think-ing—only then will you be a leader who is successful and respected by all.

39. SPRING CLEANING – NOT JUST FOR YOUR HOUSE

For a moment, cast aside the emotional baggage that may be weighing you down. Lighten your load of worries, excuses, and mistakes. Smile that a new day has sprung.

Think about what the season of spring means to you. For me, the sun is warmer, the sky is brighter, and an opportunity to begin anew awaits each of us. It is time for a little spring-cleaning of not just windows and rooms, but also of mind and heart. Let us all replenish the good and discard the unhealthy in our lives. To do so begins with attitude and the self-discipline to make it a positive one. It is the primary utensil to be used in the cleaning process. Subsequently, reinforcing the core values you stand for and believe in is essential to putting that spring back in your step.

As spring is a rebirth of the environment around us, take part in the splendor of renewing what is wonderful about you, your family, and those you impact every day. What aspects of your life need a little cleaning? Relationships, values, balance, patience, mind, body, and spirit are all facets of life that need a little dusting off and polishing once in a while. Forgiveness and establishing goals for your project are the two primary cleaning agents.

To forgive personal failures, those who have hurt you, and any unhealthy environment around you is vital to a thorough cleaning. Establishing the goals of the cleanup process provides direction and structure for the undertaking at hand. Personal accountability is the action step that validates a genuine positive attitude and the values you wish to exemplify. Not taking ownership for who you are, the life you have created, and the changes you would like to make is equivalent to expecting the house to clean itself.

DO THE TOUGH WORK

Successful spring-cleaning requires time, commitment, energy, self-discipline, and perseverance just as successful personal growth requires. It takes elbow grease and at times getting on your hands and knees to really do it correctly. It is never easy, and it should not be, for life is too precious and important to do a half-baked job. If you find yourself emotionally stuck in the basement, realize you have others who love and respect you and want you to come up and enjoy the sunroom. A proper attitude, combined with a solid set of core values and taking ownership for the implementation of those values, is a formula for greater self-respect.

Self-respect is also achieved when you learn from yesterday and apply that knowledge today for a better tomorrow. How many individuals do you know who leave their house a mess, and then generate excuses why the task to clean is too difficult and too tedious? The result is a home that deteriorates in quality, declines in value, and is neither comfortable nor enjoyable to live in. The same occurs when you procrastinate in cleaning up any mess in your life. Your life deteriorates, you decline in value, and you are probably not too comfortable, nor enjoyable, to be around.

Personal honesty is the acknowledgement that an initial cleanup is needed. To deny a needed change from the status quo is detrimental to your overall well being, both personally and professionally. As spring-cleaning creates more order in the home, emotional spring-cleaning creates greater balance in your life. Disorganization and a lack of balance foster additional stress and diminish personal value and motivation. Without spring-cleaning, how can you get your house/life in order?

Attitude, accountability, self-respect, personal honesty, and balance all contribute to the development of an effective person and a principled leader. They establish a core of solid character and an example to be looked upon favorably by yourself and others. As the aftermath of spring-cleaning your home brings with it a sense of accomplishment and pride, the aftermath of the attentive cleanup to any mess in your life is no different. Take a deep breath and celebrate when the cleanup is complete, and relish in knowing that even warmer days and brighter skies are ahead. Happy Spring Cleaning!

40. PASSION – LIFE'S LITTLE SPARK

When was the last time you were genuinely passionate about something? Was it related to your work or your personal life? Did it revolve around yourself or others? There is rarely a greater feeling of excitement than when your heart and soul are part of something you truly believe in and desire—something you know can make a positive difference in the world around you.

Passion is defined as "strong and barely controllable emotion, a state of outburst of such emotion, an intense desire or enthusiasm for something." Passion is the spark that ignites the fuel to power you to the fulfillment of your aspirations. The fruition of a cause or desire you are passionate about results in an expression of joy and happiness that is unsurpassed. The thrill of victory and the agony of defeat demonstrate how powerful passion can be in regard to human emotion.

Without passion there is apathy and boredom, both of which stifle personal and professional growth. We have all met individuals who are miserable, dislike their job, distrust everyone, and in turn display their personal dissatisfaction through their negativity, doubtfulness, excuse making, and destructive behavior. In many cases, the destructive behavior tends to be directed toward the people that matter most in their lives, usually their family and friends.

However, there should be caution with passion as well. Passion for passion's sake can be dangerous if there is no thoughtful consideration in regard to what the outcome of that passion may be. Passion can be self-serving in a healthy way, but when passion for something or someone destroys those around you, the dark side of passion is revealed. Passion for self-centered desires at the expense of others exposes an inner core of destructive character traits, primarily a lack of personal accountability and personal honesty. Healthy passion is never irresponsible and should always be an honest reflection of the values that comprise the individual.

It is also important to understand there is a difference between passion and anger. Anger transcends passion when in the course of being passionate, spontaneous verbal or physical abuse becomes apparent. Passion in combination with professionalism (emotional patience), integrity, honesty, accountability, and respect is a formula for true achievement. Genuine passion is also motivating for others to witness and be a part of. It generates a level of excitement, energy, and enthusiasm that is not normally experienced during our daily lives.

IGNITE YOUR PASSION

Much of our passion is bred in the core values we believe in. The issues, topics, and people that create internal passion are related to how they align with, or diverge from, our core values. A leader who is passionate about a core value they believe in will develop a following of similar core valued people. Thus, a collective desire for something is initiated.

A common thread of feedback I receive following my speaking engagements is the recognition of the passion I have in the delivery of my message. I am always appreciative of that feedback, and I promise to those I inspire and myself that if I ever lose the passion for what I do, I will never conduct another seminar. To not speak from the heart would be unfair to myself and the people I share my message with.

Five matches to ignite the spark of passion in your life include:

- Revisit and redefine the core values in your life that stimulate interest and excitement. They may include honesty, perseverance, integrity, and family.

- Find and connect with those who share your common values. Immediately there will be an increase in personal value because others are validating the essence of who you are.

- Attach those common values to a cause, a desire, or a dream you wish to be a part of, and initiate taking the steps to be involved in the process of making it come to fruition.

- Stay on a path of purpose that is ethical and contributes to the betterment of yourself and those around you.

- Anticipate how fun it will be to celebrate the rediscovery of passion in your life, and to continually enjoy a level of vigor in all you do.

You are the one in charge of today and tomorrow, and passion for what you love and what you wish for should forever be a part of what it means to live a life of fullness and purpose.

41. SUSCEPTIBILITY – HOW EASILY TEMPTED ARE YOU?

Here's an idea I'd like to tempt you with: How about you consider making yourself less susceptible to self-centered desires and more attentive to selfless acts of being thoughtful and respectful toward others?

Have you ever been tempted? Of course. We all have. Temptation is defined as "a desire to do something, esp. something wrong or unwise." How susceptible are you to temptation, and where does the personal strength and self-discipline reside to thwart such a destructive force? Susceptible is defined as "likely or liable to be influenced or harmed by a particular thing." The more susceptible you are to the perceived needs you have, the more likely temptation will succeed in drawing you ever closer to self-destructive behavior. What are those needs that attract temptation? They are the reflection of our personal dysfunctions and weaknesses—our vulnerabilities.

The catalyst that stimulates an attraction toward any temptation is the notion that the self will benefit. For example, if you have a need for attention, you will be more susceptible to the temptation of behaving in a destructive way to acquire that attention. It may be as simple as taking a dare from a friend or participating in a risky behavior. Similarly, if you lack self-respect, you are more susceptible to the temptation of destructive behavior to prove to others you are valuable. You might be tempted to participate in greed, lust, or the craving for power, but what are the root causes that make you susceptible to those temptations? Are you insecure with your own fiscal state of affairs, self-respect, or self-confidence?

It is the follow through to temptation resulting in personal destruction that is a reflection of personal insecurity. Anyone with a healthy personal value structure in place realizes when a temptation presents itself that is in violation of those values. Is your insecurity or need for something from the outside more important than what you stand for and believe in on the inside?

STAY TRUE TO YOUR CORE

The ability to become less susceptible to temptation rests in the understanding and strength to implement the core values you believe define the most important elements of your character. If a true core value of yours is honesty, then your ability and commitment to live that value will determine how susceptible you are to being dishonest. The most important question to ask is, "How will succumbing to any temptation affect those around me, in particular my family and friends?" The redirection of thought from self-centeredness to selflessness is the initial key to dismantling temptation. The reward in rejecting temptation is increased self-discipline and a higher level of personal confidence.

Five steps to reducing your susceptibility to unhealthy temptations include:

- Revisit, update, and redefine the core values that form the substance of your character and what you stand for and believe in. If you lack an understanding of those values you will be in a weakened state when confronting destructive temptations.

- Use common sense in analyzing the situation you may be confronted with. If you have any type of positive value base, you do not have to be a rocket scientist to know right from wrong. Just say "no."

- Behave in a consistent way that reinforces your core values. Every time you do, it enhances self-respect and strength of character. If you have no values to base your behavior upon, there is no way you can earn any degree of self-respect or self-confidence. Why? You have neither self-identity nor a personal understanding of you.

- If you have a history of being susceptible to particular temptations, make a concerted effort not to put yourself in situations that invite those temptations.

- Ask yourself, "What is most important in my life, and what do I wish to be remembered for? Is it what I have taken or what I have given? What I have done for myself or what I have done for others?"

We may never know what tomorrow may bring, but we will all be living in the future, so we might as well make it a future worth living.

42. WILLPOWER – AN AGELESS ATTRIBUTE

The motivation to achieve personally and professionally can be a daunting task. The demands of life and the distractions that occur in the process of maintaining life balance can be a formidable challenge. Your willpower to drive forward directly relates to your strength of character and to your foundation of self-respect. While your strength of character provides a platform for your life's purpose, your self-respect generates your level of confidence to accomplish that purpose.

How much do you believe in yourself and the principles you stand for? How strong is your willpower to work hard, parent effectively, live an honorable and personally honest life, and stay healthy? Have you given up, or do you believe you have a purpose? Do you have the ability to continue to contribute to yourself, as well as to those around you? Finally, what are the roots to a resilient willpower and how do you harness it?

Willpower is defined as "the ability to carry out one's decisions, wishes, or plans; strength of mind; self-control." To harness the will to be resilient is dependent on the core values that motivate you to live a purposeful life. Without a foundation of core values that sustain you, your life will have little direction. Your attitude will be negatively impacted, and therefore your will to persevere diminished. As Mahatma Gandhi said, "Strength does not come from physical capacity. It comes from an indomitable will."

Ethical core values also develop the willpower to cast away temptation and defeat elements of evil. If you genuinely believe that honesty is a vital characteristic of a fulfilled purpose, then you will have greater willpower to avoid the temptation of dishonesty. If integrity is a core value that you genuinely believe defines who you are, then you will have greater willpower to fend off situations that might compromise your integrity. It is having the willpower to do the right thing over any evil temptation that continually builds your character and self-respect.

How many individuals who succumbed to unethical or unhealthy temptations are proud of themselves? How many are free in thought and spirit in the aftermath of forfeiting the willpower to do the right thing? Are you exercising your willpower on a daily basis in order to reinforce the core values you believe in? Do you have the willpower to set that example?

CLAIM YOUR POWER

The American Psychological Association expanded on the basic definition of willpower by including more specific behavioral applications. These include:

- The ability to delay gratification, resisting short-term temptations in order to meet long-term goals.

- The capacity to override an unwanted thought, feeling, or impulse.

- The ability to employ a "cool" cognitive system of behavior rather than a "hot" emotional system.

- Conscious, effortful regulation of the self by the self.

- A limited resource capable of being depleted.

I believe we all have the potential to develop the willpower to push us toward the accomplishment of our desires and aspirations. It is the continuous process of putting into practice the core values you believe in that generates that power. It is also making a concerted effort to ask yourself in harmful and tempting situations, "What will be the consequences in lacking the will power to do the right thing? What hurt might I cause others or myself if I lack that willpower?"

As former British Prime Minister Benjamin Disraeli said, "Nothing can withstand the power of the human will if it is willing to stake its very existence to the extent of its purpose."

43. AMBITION – A MOTIVATION TO EXCEL

When you hear someone is ambitious, what comes to mind? Do you evaluate it positively or negatively? Do you see it as a self-centered and egotistical attribute, or one that is selfless and thoughtful? What is the motive behind ambition? Is it to serve and elevate the self, or an outcome that is beneficial to the many?

Ambition is critical to a positive future. To be ambitious substantiates a degree of purpose in your life and a willingness to move forward in the development of who you are personally and professionally. Without ambition there is no fuel to power the engine that moves you toward the accomplishment of your goals and ultimate success. What are your goals, and do they provide ambition for you to succeed? Do you have goals that do not require ambition? It is doubtful, because a goal is the catalyst behind any ambition.

When you wake up each morning do you have something to look forward to? If so, you have a goal and therefore the ambition to see it come to fruition. Ambition is defined as "an earnest desire for some type of achievement or distinction, as power, honor, fame, or wealth, and the willingness to strive for its attainment: the object, state or result desired or sought after." Earnest is the key word defined as "serious in intention, purpose and effort." Without an earnest desire, what you may have ambition to accomplish is a pipe dream, because you lack the necessary drive to get there.

Unethical ambition is, and has been, one of the most destructive human forces in history. In contrast, ethical ambition is and has been, one of the most powerful forces behind great human achievement. When your ambition is executed by ethical and righteous means, the benefit of your accomplishment will extend beyond the self. There is a fine line between selfless and self-centered ambition, and keeping the eye on that line is imperative to the meaningful and enduring success of that ambition.

HOW DO YOU VIEW AMBITION?

Often, when we hear of ambition we tend to think of acquiring possessions and how unscrupulous people may have attained those possessions. However, you can be ambitious about having a happy, harmonious, and successful family. You can be ambitious about staying healthy and setting a proper example in all you do. You can be ambitious about being a person of integrity and thoughtfulness. You can be ambitious about having made a positive difference in those around you.

Therefore, look at ambition as being one of the most energizing and worthwhile attributes you possess. It is not bad to strive for something you desire and believe in. It is only when ambition blinds the soul and tarnishes the heart that negative consequences occur and a society is damaged. Without those with ambition for freedom, equality, justice, peace, and human rights, the world would be a different place.

There are many figures, historically and present day, who had and have evil ambitions. I am hopeful there will always be those who defeat those who have that propensity toward evil. Celebrate being ambitious for goodness. Encourage and support yourself and those who have the ambition to do good things for people and society. As Abraham Lincoln stated, "I would rather be a little nobody, than to be an evil somebody." The platform for ethical ambition stems from an ethical platform of core values. Honesty, integrity, character, and humility are several that personally come to mind. Is what you strive for each day in alignment with the values you believe in? Is the end result only to benefit the self or does it have a greater purpose?

The ambition of others surrounds us each day. Do you have the ability to decipher between ambition of goodness and evil? Your frame of reference and the accuracy of your assessment will depend on how you live your own life. What might that self-assessment be? As Napoleon Bonaparte said, "Great ambition is the passion of a great character. Those endowed with it may perform very good or very bad acts. All depends on the principles which direct them." Enjoy the fulfillment of striving for goodness over evil, and take pride in having the ambition to accomplish each goal you set for yourself.

SECTION SIX

WISDOM

By three methods we may learn wisdom: First, by reflection,
which is noblest; Second, by imitation, which is easiest; and third
by experience, which is the bitterest.
– Confucius

How wonderful would it be to be wise? To have the wisdom to understand and channel your life's experiences into a logical sequence of existence would be an amazing achievement. To have the wisdom to integrate the world around you and understand how it applies to the meaning of your own life would generate an unparalleled sense of purpose.

Education added to experience generates wisdom. Wisdom is validated by the encounters we have with our environment and one another. A wise person has the ability to intellectually digest their surroundings emotionally, physically, and environmentally for the purpose of generating understanding. A wise person is also an intuitive person. Upon reflection, there are many times you have gone with and trusted your intuition, and you were right. How did you know? Wisdom is developed, and yet there is evidence of superior intellect and thought that is hard to explain.

Where does our wisdom come from? Wisdom is defined as "the quality of having experience, knowledge, and good judgment; the quality of being wise; the soundness of an action or decision with regard to the application of such experience, knowledge and good judgment; the body of knowledge and principles that develops within a specified society or period." The more you know, and the more you experience, most likely the wiser you will be. To ignore an opportunity to experience or learn is a choice, but hopefully a choice you rarely make. There is an infinite abundance of knowledge and discovery to be had, and it is what makes life worth living.

The principles in this section are designed to further engage you in your own personal discovery and stimulate an understanding of the wisdom you possess. It is always invigorating to encounter a wise individual—one who shares their experience and stimulates thought that inspires you to reach higher levels of understanding. You possess wisdom, and truly wise individuals are those who know the benefit in sharing their wisdom with others.

The greater the ability you have to integrate your education, experience, and core values you believe in within the world around you, the wiser you will be. A wise person will understand how important the principles of character, decency, gratitude, humility, and self-discipline are to living a purposeful and respectful life. Reflect on the wisdom and goodness that rests inside of you, and take the time to share your wisdom and goodness with others, for it is always remembered.

44. ACHIEVEMENT – CELEBRATE THE HUMAN SPIRIT

There is little that comes close to the excitement and satisfaction of human achievement. Yet, there is a prevailing wind that achieving success is being stifled by the continuous emphasis on class differences and political maneuvering for the purpose of gaining power. An energy promulgating the need to compare, rather than inspiring one to individually excel, is socially debilitating. It is always easier to use the achievement of others as an excuse to justify your own inabilities than it is to take the initiative to learn and apply the principles that created that achievement. Of course, I am referring to those who achieve ethically and fairly, and not at the expense of others. In addition, I am not including those who are genuinely in need and have been victimized. I am referring to the pseudo victims who have the capability to achieve but decide to use those who do achieve as their excuse for not achieving themselves.

It is destructive to a society when more attention is paid to having been the victim, rather than encouraging a path of self-reliance, self-respect, and personal accountability. The backbone of human achievement has been independence, never dependence. It's been a focus on freedom, never tyranny, and one of free markets, never controlled markets. These principled applications are far from perfect, and there have been many instances of unfairness and injustice throughout history, but it has been those ideals that have created, for this nation, the greatest innovation, creativity, and achievement the world has ever seen. Human achievement should never be frowned upon and never used to divide its citizenry, but rather a catalyst to inspire every citizen to strive toward their own potential and ultimate achievement.

THE GREATEST SUCCESS

Achievement is defined as "something accomplished, especially by superior ability, special effort, great courage, etc., a great or heroic deed." I may be an idealist, but I believe everyone has the ability to achieve if the resources and education are available. In this nation, with all of its abundance, there is no excuse not to promote that potential in all of us. The foundation of any achievement stems from an awareness of the values, skills, and characteristics that it takes to achieve. Personal accountability, awareness, and acceptance are the cornerstones to begin to understand those values, skills, and characteristics. Additionally, confidence and self-respect are the result of acting on those cornerstones. Without a foundation of what you stand for and believe in, your core values, the soul is lost. Without confidence and self-respect, the mind is discouraged and the spirit depressed. Ayn Rand stated, "Happiness is that state of consciousness which proceeds from the achievement of one's values."

It is not someone or something that limits your own achievements. It is the understanding that it ultimately comes down to your attitude and your desire to break away from the old and strive for the new. As Helen Keller said, "Optimism is the faith that leads to achievement. Nothing can be done without hope and confidence."

There are those who can influence you both positively and negatively. Ultimately, it is your responsibility to embrace the challenge to achieve, or to live as a victim and believe some outside entity will rescue you from yourself. The answer to your ultimate happiness never resides outside; rather, it is an internal sense of living a life that is honest, honorable, and aligned with what you project to the outside. Stuff may suppress having to take accountability for your life, but it will never fill the void of being personally dishonest.

To achieve is to reveal who you are to yourself and the potential you possess to be a successful person. Success is different for everyone, but it is the individual that defines it for themselves, not a corporation, not reality television, not your friends, and not the government. The beauty of who we are as a people has always been the belief that the sky is the limit of what is possible.

Does anyone honestly believe that to devalue achievement motivates anyone? Achievement will never be celebrated when it is limited, dictated, and controlled. It will breed apathy, a lack of work ethic, decreased morale, dependency, and little motivation for an individual to take the initiative to do anything different. As author Denis Waitley said, "The most splendid achievement of all is the constant striving to surpass yourself and to be worthy of your own approval."

45. THE CHALLENGE OF PERCEPTION

What type of person do others perceive you as being? Do they perceive you as being kind, compassionate, sensitive, arrogant, competitive, self-centered, empathetic, wise, or aloof, etc? Why are there occasional misunderstandings between self-perception and another's perception of you? Certainly what you say, the tone and inflection of your voice, your body language, and how you look can be interpreted different ways by different people. There are times I am challenged with my own self-perception of what I convey versus how it is perceived and interpreted by others. Have you ever said to someone, "I did not mean it that way?"

The accuracy of your perception of another, or another's perception of you, is directly correlated with the level of maturity, life experience, intellect, open-mindedness, and emotional stability each person possesses. As the renowned Canadian novelist Robertson Davies stated, "The eye sees only what the mind is prepared to comprehend."

Misinterpretation of another can be the result of attempting to place your own belief system and way of doing things on another. It is important to remember not everyone is like you. There are many times your own insecurities influence how your perceive others. For example, if someone shares an opinion in regard to the lack of personal responsibility that exists in our society today, and you know you have not been personally responsible in your own life, the more likely you are to interpret that opinion as being offensive rather than an objective opinion. Flipping the coin, if you share an opinion that triggers discomfort or anger in another, their perception of you will be very different as compared to an opinion you share that positively validates their own thoughts and opinions. As the founder of analytical psychology Carl Jung stated, "Everything that irritates us about others can lead us to an understanding of ourselves."

DO YOU SEE WHAT I SEE?

The more insecure you are with yourself, the more subjective you will be, and therefore less accurate in your perception of others. Why? You allow emotion to override objective analysis. The greater the insecurity, the more vulnerable you are to an emotional trigger. In addition, the more you protect your insecurities, the more defensive you will be to those who threaten that protection. As Hans Margolius stated, "Only in quiet waters things mirror themselves undistorted. Only in a quiet mind is adequate perception of the world."

One behavior not difficult to perceive accurately is hypocrisy. It is the ultimate destroyer of one's character. To say one thing and behave differently reveals to all a personally dishonest person. The establishment of a formal set of core values in your life is essential to creating consistency in behavior. The less you know what those core values are, and the less you implement them, the more susceptible you are to being inconsistent and therefore hypocritical. The belief and executing of your core values also provide a greater level of emotional security. As a result, you are more likely to be objective in your perception, rather than emotionally judgmental of another.

In regard to the ability to be accurately perceptive, we should all strive to be perspicacious. It is not only my word for you for the day, but a great trait to acquire. Perspicacious is defined as "having keen mental perception and understanding; discerning; to exhibit perspicacious judgment." Some synonyms include acute, astute, discerning, penetrating, percipient, sagacious, and sharp-witted. Perspicacity is achieved through experience, education, and a willingness to be empathetic to those around you. It is also achieved through living a consistently ethical life, allowing greater discernment when witnessing less than honorable behavior.

Empathy is defined as "the intellectual identification with or vicarious experiencing of the feelings, thoughts, or attitudes of another." To be empathetically perceptive is an ideal opportunity to be non-judgmental of another, and also perspicacious. It does not mean you retreat from the core values you believe in, but it does allow you to think before you react and temper your response. As Leonardo Da Vinci so simply stated, "All our knowledge is the offspring of our perceptions." Enjoy the opportunity to practice being perspicacious and becoming more acutely perceptive of the people and the world around you.

46. INSECURITY – A MENACE TO SUCCESS AND HAPPINESS

What are you insecure about? How secure are you with who you are, what you look like, your attributes, your shortcomings, the content of your character, and your virtues? Do you have a moral compass in life that you follow? Does that compass only guide you? Do you act on the directions that compass provides you? Do you use your insecurities as an excuse for a lack of achievement, or do you recognize that your insecurities are actually a stimulus to improve and become a better you?

Insecurity is the flashing warning sign in your life telling you to research the roots of that insecurity and take the necessary actions to minimize its impact. Insecure is defined as "(of a person) not confident or assured; uncertain and anxious." Anxious is a key word for it is the physical and emotional catalyst to recognizing insecurity exists. Anxious is defined as "experiencing worry, unease, or nervousness, typically about an imminent event or something with an uncertain outcome." Yikes! I just realized I might need to practice a little bit better what I preach.

Where do our insecurities originate? Certainly our upbringing, relationships, failures, social expectations and environment all contribute to the development of them. For example, if you are insecure about how you look, where does that insecurity stem from? If it is from the expectations of a superficial society, then maybe there is nothing to be insecure about. Take the makeup artists and the hair stylists away from the so-called beauty queens and kings and famous celebrities, and you will realize that perception is not always reality.

However, there is a responsibility that comes with insecurity. The responsibility is taking ownership for insecurity created by your own actions. If you are insecure about your body, yet you do not manage your weight and health effectively, you are not taking responsibility for the issue at hand. It then becomes much easier to use that insecurity as an excuse rather than a motivation to improve.

BEWARE THE DOWNWARD PATH

There is a direct correlation between guilt, insecurity, and regret. Guilt drives us to be unsure about the life path we have taken and the decisions we have made. As a result, the more insecure we are about ourselves. This culminates into regret that is emotionally draining and sustains a focus on a gloomy past, rather than a bright future. It is not who you are that holds you back; it is who you think you are not.

The more you are irresponsible for your insecurities, the more destructive you become. It transcends to the blaming of everything and everyone around you for your own lack of accomplishment and success. Envy, jealousy, bigotry, and prejudice are the ultimate behaviors that demonstrate how deep someone's insecurities can become. As Oliver Wendell Holmes, Jr. stated, "The mind of a bigot is like the pupil of the eye. The more light you shine on it, the more it will contract."

How do you right the ship? First, what is the foundation for what you stand for and believe in? Second, what are the characteristics and principles that you believe create a good and decent person? These answered collectively form the very core values that provide a greater deal of security moving forward with your life and the decisions you will make. Insecurity tends to be more of a subjective opinion of your own sense of self-worth rather than being based on actual fact. Without a foundation of values to build your self-worth around, the more vulnerable you are to your perceived insecurities.

Other steps to overcome include:

- Be proactive, not reactive, when you recognize insecurity exists.

- Learn to trust yourself and the abilities you have. There are more wonderful things about you than you may realize.

- Forgive yourself. We all make mistakes.

- Surround yourself with people who lift you up, not pull you down. Emulate positive not negative behaviors.

- Realize everyone has insecurities; however, it is a choice whether you allow them to control you and how you feel.

- Do not host an internal pity party. Life is too short.

As the classic quote from Eleanor Roosevelt states, "No one can make you feel inferior without your consent."

47. LIVING UP TO YOUR POTENTIAL – IT'S NEVER TOO LATE

Do you desire to be more successful in life than you currently are? I would hope you do, as it provides an inspiration to wake up each day. To believe you have the potential to improve your life is imperative for being motivated to excel and optimistic about your future. If you do not believe in your potential to be a better you, why get out of bed?

Potential is defined as "latent qualities or abilities that may be developed and lead to future success or usefulness," "having or showing the capacity to become or develop into something in the future." A strong belief in your potential first stems from having a foundation of personal core values that you strive to implement daily. Without the existence of core values there is no path to guide how you will ethically live up to that potential.

Core values provide the framework to align what you strive for with who you are and what you believe in. Living your core values is the cornerstone for building a positive attitude, and attitude is a reflection of your self-respect. Therefore, a positive attitude plus self-respect is a formula for a better you.

What areas of your life would you like to improve upon? When was the last time you asked yourself such a question? We all have the potential to become better individuals. Although there may be some physical and psychological restraints to the extent of that improvement, making the choice to delve into your untapped skills and talents is a positive adventure in itself. For example, how enjoyable might it be to start an art class, take piano lessons, join an outdoors club, take on a new physical challenge, be further involved in your community, take up a cause, or study a new subject matter of interest? There is always the potential for failure, but more important is the potential for success. As Joseph Campbell stated, "The cave you fear to enter holds the treasure you seek."

SEIZE YOUR OPPORTUNITIES

Expecting something in your life to change and improve by always doing the same thing is a definition for insanity. Life has a way of offering to all of us the opportunity to discover a new experience and gain a new perspective. Are you one to recognize and grab on to those opportunities, or are you one to expect someone else to do it for you? If it is the latter, say hello to believing you are entitled. Entitlement destroys human potential because there is no perceived effort needed to what one believes he or she deserves. Without effort there is no potential for personal or professional growth. In physics, potential is the quantity determining the energy of mass in a gravitational field. Life is your gravitational field, you are the mass, and without substantial energy there is little potential for further success. As Winston Churchill said, "Continuous effort—not strength or intelligence—is the key to unlocking our potential."

Self-esteem is defined as "pride in one's self," and pride is defined as "dignity and self-respect." Living up to your potential, as with self-esteem, is earned not given. It is essential to instill this principle of understanding in your children for they will gain a better appreciation for themselves when they realize they have earned their accomplishments. An "everybody gets a trophy" type of mentorship does little to encourage a high degree of effort by those being mentored. It stifles what it means to live up to your potential. As with any fulfilling endeavor, the effort you put in directly correlates with the level of reward that is returned.

Seven steps to unlocking your potential include:

- Recognize what you would like to improve upon or research something new you would like to do.

- Understand your limitations and levels of expectation.

- Take everything in moderation; do not bite off more than you can chew.

- Prepare properly to prevent poor performance.

- Pace yourself, yet proceed with enthusiasm.

- Be resolute in your commitment to the new endeavor; quitting is not an option.

- Celebrate the accomplishment and how it has contributed to your zest to live life to the fullest.

As Helen Keller so poignantly noted, "I am only one, but still I am one. I cannot do everything, but still I can do something; and because I cannot do everything, I will not refuse to do something that I can do."

48. THE MORALITY-TECHNOLOGY DILEMMA

One constant throughout human history has been the ability of human beings to advance technologically. The advent of the wheel, printing press, electricity, automobile, telephone, television, modern weaponry, computers, and the Internet are all examples. What has also been constant is society's meager attempt to keep pace, align, and apply morality with technological advancement.

The splitting of the atom and the development of the Internet has changed the world forever, but it has also forced a new examination of the moral consequences of such change. From the ability to annihilate millions with the push of a button to the capacity to communicate with others anywhere, anytime, and explore every facet of human information forces an expansive understanding of right and wrong behaviors. The advent of texting and social networking only adds to the complexity of what is appropriate communication. It may provide the opportunity to access friends present and past, but it also invites the potential for deceit and irresponsible behavior.

Technology has opened many avenues to explore our existence and human relationships, but with it comes an added responsibility to ensure we behave in a respectful and dignified way toward others. Ironically, Albert Einstein quoted, "It has become appallingly obvious that our technology has exceeded our humanity."

What does it mean to be moral? Morality is defined as "principles concerning the distinction between right and wrong or good and bad behavior." Based on religion, culture, and social norms that definition can be left to much interpretation in regard to what is right and wrong behavior. I define morality in my life as how I treat another human being, and I believe we should treat one another with dignity and respect. It is a behavioral practice I attempt to emulate every day.

On a positive note, technology has forced us to evaluate even further what is appropriate and inappropriate behavior. Each day we are exposed to information relating to human behavior that creates discussion and examination. John Naisbitt stated, "The most exciting breakthroughs of the 21st century will not occur because of technology, but because of an expanding concept of what it means to be human."

THE GREATEST DANGERS

Technology can also create insensitivity toward human suffering and the feelings of others. When our children participate in video games of violence, murder, and human mutilation so graphic, there is no possible way it adds to an increased understanding of the sanctity of life or what it means to be compassionate. When a drone pilot can drop munitions while sitting in a chair thousands of miles away from the target, execute the murder of humans, proceed home for dinner that evening, and repeat that scenario consistently, there is no doubt that a desensitizing of human anguish occurs. As technology continues to advance it is imperative to be mindful of the influence technology has on our children's interpretation of right and wrong. It is the core values of a parent and family that provide the foundation to give moral guidance to those around us. Without core values to mold and discipline behavior, the influence of technology will.

The greatest danger in modern technology isn't that machines will begin to think like people, but that people will begin to think like machines. As we shop for the next new technological marvel, let us also shop for the time to enjoy one another and the spirit that comes with thinking a bit more of others than ourselves. As you are sitting around the dinner table some evening with those you love ask the following two questions: "What aspects of morality has technology impacted both positively and negatively?" and "What does it mean to be human, and is there a recent experience that ignited that human spirit in you?"

As WWII General Omar Bradley so poignantly stated, "If we continue to develop our technology without wisdom or prudence, our servant may prove to be our executioner." Never forget the moral responsibility that comes with being human. It will generate respect for life and living for generations to come.

49. THE THIRST FOR POWER – A SOCIAL CATASTROPHE

What is the lure of power, and why is individual power so important to so many? As the span of local to world events continually unfolds, it is increasingly evident how the need for power is taking precedence over human decency.

Two definitions of power are "the capacity or ability to direct or influence the behavior of others or the course of events," and "political or social authority or control." The catalyst for desiring power can be both positive and negative. When it is solely self-serving it is negative. The implementation of such control over others destroys trust, mutual respect, and efficient communication. This can wreak havoc on the effectiveness and productivity of institutions, organizations, societies, and relationships.

A person's need for power added to an individually driven agenda is a recipe for destructive and self-centered behavior. Its negative influence can easily corrode the foundation of a morally good person. Interestingly, the need for power by many individuals' stems from their own personal insecurity and the belief that dominating others will negate that insecurity. How wrong they are. We, as citizens, consistently witness the destructive aftermath of those who strive for power at the expense of colleagues, family, friends, and others.

Destructive power can dismantle the necessity for personal account-ability among those in power. They use their power to threaten those who may question a decision made or a behavior displayed. It is also interesting to observe how individuals of principle tend to pose a threat to those who use their power in an unethical or less than profes-sional manner. It may force accountability for their actions. Power can also be a cloak to cover up personal dishonesty. The requirement to be honest is suppressed when one holds power over another, because they control the potential progress of that person, family, company, community, or country.

USE YOUR POWER WISELY

Dr. Rollo May (1909-1994), a renowned American existential psychologist, defined power as "the ability to cause or prevent change." Change is the key word in the definition, because change can be a threat or a catalyst to an individual's maintaining of power. He also proposed two negative types of power, Exploitive Power and Manipulative Power. These two powers are extremely destructive. When used, it is a true indicator of one's personal and professional insecurity.

Exploitive Power is the most destructive form of power and it is when power is used "on" another. The aggressor allows the victim no options in the exchange. For example, exploitive power may be making demands on a victim while threatening his life, or a demand that if not followed through with may result in the firing of the individual.

Manipulative Power pertains to persons who are unequal in their power and resources, and is used "over" another. The person with more power influences the other's behavior. For example, in regard to human relationships, manipulative power may include unfair interactions between parent and child, manager and employee, teacher and student, therapist and client, and husband and wife. These destructive powers are also initiated when one senses a loss of control whether it is with a person or situation.

When you are not threatened by your own insecurities or the principled behavior of others, and when you live a life where healthy core values are adhered to, the necessity to use these two types of power is nullified. To exploit or manipulate another to prevent not doing the right thing is the worst expression of destructive power. When in their own mind superiority justifies abuse and unethical behavior, it is a disgrace. It is a true sign of a lack of genuine character, leadership, and personal honesty.

There is no doubt that power can be used for the greater good. It is an important element in creating change, with the hope of improving our quality of life, workplace, and society. It is ideal to think that all leaders would use their power in a selfless and caring manner for the benefit of others, but for those of us in positions of leadership and power there is no justification to exploit, manipulate, and threaten those who are subordinate to us. It is an example of our own weaknesses, rather than displaying the strengths of an effective leader.

50. SERENDIPITY – NOT JUST BY CHANCE

Serendipity is defined as "the occurrence and development of events by chance in a happy or beneficial way." Luck is defined as "success or failure apparently brought by chance rather than through one's own actions." Is there such a thing as luck, or is it an extension of what we do every day? Both definitions include the word "chance," which brings into question, are we in control of the occurrences that surround us? Are the results of luck and serendipity related to coincidence?

Coincidence is defined as "a remarkable concurrence of events or circumstances without apparent causal connection." Why do some win raffles and others do not? Why do some appear to be at the right time and place for opportunity and others are not? Why do bad things happen to good people, or why does tragedy befall so many? How is it we meet strangers and there is a mutual connection? How is it we were just thinking about something or someone and an hour later we experience that thing or run into that someone? I cannot begin to count the number of times I have thought of a client, the scheduling of an event, a question I needed to ask, or correspondence I had to create, and moments later the phone rings or I receive an email and it is the person or item I was thinking about.

A REASON FOR EVERYTHING

Beyond the isolated uncontrolled global events, coincidence is created by the energy and behavior we exude to the world around us. The kinder you are, the more kindness is returned. The more respect you demonstrate, the more respect is returned. The less you hang around negative, self-centered people, the less those people enter your life. Coincidence? Consistently you attract the energy and thoughts you project. It is a collection of those positive actions that increase the "chance" for serendipity and the experience of luck in our lives.

Notice that "failure" was included in the definition of luck. If you display destructive, dishonest, self-centered, negative behavior, the "chance" for failure is increased. It is not coincidental that failure or success occurs as a result of our actions; it is directly related. There is always a causal connection between behavior and occurrence in regard to personal character, performance, relationships, and self-respect. It is not by chance as a result of lying you destroy a relationship. It is not by chance if you neglect your health you will become ill. It is not by chance if you procrastinate the quality of your work will diminish. It is not by chance if you are not accountable the chance for genuine happiness is remote. It is not by chance if you are fiscally irresponsible you will have financial difficulties.

As mentioned, there are the unexplainable occurrences and events, but those are rare as compared to the day-to-day cause and effect we create for ourselves. There are common occurrences in the midst of common thought, and the more common thought reflects your core values, the more you attract similar core valued people into your life. I share with my audiences that I believe I am supposed to be there with and for them in regard to sharing the "No Excuse!" message. It may be for a few, it may be for many, but it is not chance that I am hired at that time, for that event, at that place. I thoroughly enjoy serendipity, but there is common energy behind every serendipitous moment.

Reflect and celebrate serendipity and the positive experience of luck and coincidence because you are a part of that occurrence. Why not believe that to be true? There is nothing to lose, only tremendous joy believing that you are a part of your own future and purpose. It is emotionally and physically healthier to believe the life you lead and the positive results that occur are in some way a result of your own efforts. Although tomorrow may bring sorrow, a loss, or a tragedy, live with the belief that wonderful things can and will happen to you. As you live today create your own serendipity, your own luck, and your own coincidence by delivering goodness and demonstrating selflessness to those around you. Each day is a gift, and each day is an opportunity to create what kind of gift you unwrap.

51. SOCIAL INDEPENDENCE – AN IMPETUS FOR HUMAN ACHIEVEMENT

Why is being independent in thought and action so important to the sustainability and evolution of the human spirit? As a healthy adult, what happens to individual self-respect if you become dependent on someone or something else to make decisions for you? How is personal responsibility impacted by dependency? What happens to a society when the people no longer have an independent say in the direction of their future? These are questions that should not be answered exclusively by politicians, but questions each of us should examine and reflect on for ourselves. There is presently an increased competition between self-determination and determination by others. Which one would you prefer to be the winner? Personally, I do not want someone else determining what my life can and will be.

Independent is defined as "free from outside control; not depending on another's authority," "not depending on another for livelihood or subsistence," "capable of thinking or acting for oneself." Would anyone reading those defining statements want the opposite for their life's future? I am not suggesting we neglect those in need nor disobey laws that protect our citizenry, but I am suggesting we have a responsibility to ensure dependency is not forced upon community and individuals. It is and has been social independence, partnered with independent thinking, that has ignited innovation, creativity, and societal progress.

Historically, independent thinkers have spurred the greatest periods of human achievement. The onset of the Renaissance where independent thinking bred the likes of Leonardo da Vinci, Michelangelo, Galileo, Issac Newton, and explorer Amerigo Vespucci is just one example. It is, and has been, the independent thinking in America that has spawned progress scientifically, economically, and socially, which is still the envy of many who seek an opportunity to trigger their own human potential.

In contrast, the periods of history where independent thought was persecuted, human ingenuity, innovation, and progress were stifled. The Soviet Union's blanket of communism would be a prominent example in recent Western history of the deleterious effect of social dependency.

Many of those once independent nations became irrelevant in contributing to the advancement of global progress. It is the freedom to make choices that is the foundation for human ingenuity. If we no longer have the right to choose, and choices are made for us, why would anyone be motivated to explore and capitalize on their capabilities? The incentive to achieve is lost because there is no emotional, physical, or financial reward for any effort made. Creating a dependent mindset deteriorates entrepreneurial spirit and breeds mediocrity.

STAND UP FOR YOUR INDEPENDENCE
Another limitation that prevails from social dependency is a narrowing of perceptions and viewpoints. If controls are placed on what one may say and achieve, then say farewell to creativity, innovation, and the allowance of difference in thought. When societal leadership begins to limit our rights to exercise the basic freedoms that created America's world leadership in the first place, we are all harmed. Our freedom to be independent should not be debated by any political entity; it should be their unified responsibility to help preserve it. An independent way of life is not an issue; it is a fundamental right of freedom.

Finally, social dependency depletes individual uniqueness and social diversity. It may appear that it invites acceptance of a more diverse society, but in actuality it generates just the opposite. Is it healthy to have everyone like everyone else? It is the diversity of our independent thinking, and the acceptance of difference, that creates true diversity. I believe in equality of rights among all human beings, but not the creation of an equal society where everyone is expected to think a certain way, be dependent on some governmental entity to care for them, and be limited to what their potential for greatness may be.

Social dependency deteriorates individual value and self-respect, makes an individual responsible to a governing body not themselves, and determines the future for its citizenry. It is responsible and healthy to debate issues and to create and pass legislation that protects and preserves our citizenry. It is not the responsibility of those in power to diminish our rights as citizens to choose and stifle us from attaining our full human potential. To tap into the talents, skills, creativity, and spirit of our humanness are what make us all distinctly human.

52. INTERDEPENDENCY – THE WEB OF ACHIEVEMENT

Ultimately, the final framework of your life will be a collection of the choices you have made and the execution of the core values you believed in. Others and circumstances may have influenced those decisions, but regardless they will have been your decisions. Throughout my writings, I have shared certain topics that focus on a particular value or behavior. It is critically important to understand it is not you alone, nor one core value or principle, that contributes to the final outcome of what your life and career will be. It is the working interdependency and the application of the many core values you believe in, in conjunction with your definitive relationships, that are the mechanism to create the life you want.

Web is defined as a complex system of interconnected elements, a network of fine threads (values) constructed by a spider (human being) from fluid secreted by its spinnerets (behavior), used to catch its prey (success). Yes, you are the web you weave and it is, and will be, your decisions that create the opportunity to catch success.

An established foundation of constructive core values is the fundamental structure that will build the life you desire. It provides a greater ability to hold yourself and others accountable because you have an understanding of what you stand for and believe in. This provides increased individual credibility and a capability to set expectations and standards for your personal behaviors and performance. When you act on the core values you believe in, you begin to develop an enhanced level of personal honesty because you are living a life that is a reflection of who you are. Additionally, an increased awareness of the importance of aligning who you are with what you project to others is established.

At that moment you become a person of integrity because you are behaving in a way consistent with your values. Combine consistency in behavior with being morally upright and you gain a higher degree of self-worth. Your self-esteem (pride in oneself, possessing dignity and self-respect) is solidified as you have earned an understanding of what is important and defines you. Subsequently, your attitude turns more positive. You are in stricter control of who you want to be, and the outside world has less influence on whether or not you put a smile on your face. This internal growth stimulates the practice of being more selfless than self-centered because you are more accepting of you.

WORKING TOGETHER FOR GOOD

Phase two of this process is the ease at which other principles are incorporated as a result of having a solid sense of self. Forgiveness becomes relevant and is more easily executed since you are less likely to allow past personal failures and hurts be used as justification to be miserable. You are now in control of the present, positive about the future, and the past no longer dictates how you feel. Again, this immediately increases your self-respect and self-worth.

Professionalism is enhanced as a result of less internal frustration and disappointment. This solid level of self-respect increases your ability to handle stress and pressure, and in turn you maintain patience and professionalism with yourself and others. It also increases personal resilience and perseverance. A stronger self is less likely to give up on a task and more likely to accomplish a task or goal at hand. You are also more motivated because you value yourself.

It is the working relationship of these many core values that generates happiness, fulfillment, and contentment in our lives. The greatest benefit of this interdependency is the ease at which our focus changes away from self-centeredness and is now directed toward others and family. When your web is strong, taut, and interconnected you have the ability to overcome the pressure exerted by others, the stressors of life, the winds of change, and those who wish to shred your web apart.

Each day is an opportunity to build a stronger web of personal and professional achievement. Let us all weave a web of gratitude, mutual respect, selflessness, generosity, humility, and compassion together. It will be a web forever strong, flexible, and enduring.

CONCLUSION

Now that you have a better understanding of how the core values of Character, Decency, Gratitude, Humility, Self-Discipline, and Wisdom play out in life, how is *your* life going to be different? What changes will you make? What new paths will you explore? What new relationships will your forge? How will you be a better person at home, at work, and in your community?

As you go forward, remember that making any type of change in life never happens overnight. It takes patience and persistence to reach the other side. However, with your core values guiding you, you can make any change you desire, and your actions can have a great impact on those around you.

Reflect on these six core values we've discussed, and start exploring other core values that are important to you. Get clear on what they mean in your life and how you will embody them. Talk about them with family and friends. The more awareness you can help bring to others about core values, the better the world will be.

Ultimately, when you live a life that reflects your core values, you'll be better equipped to overcome obstacles, achieve your goals, and attain all the success and happiness you deserve. I wish you well on your journey.

ABOUT THE AUTHOR

Internationally renowned speaker, trainer, and consultant Jay C. Rifenbary educates and motivates corporate teams and conference attendees through his world-class, on-site professional training and development seminars, workshops, and keynote speeches.

A resident of Saratoga Springs, NY, Jay is president of Rifenbary Training & Development and author of the international best-seller, *No Excuse! – Incorporating Core Values, Accountability and Balance into Your Life and Career* and *True To Your Core - Common Sense Values for Living Life to Its Fullest.*

He has provided his expertise in the areas of personal and professional core value development, leadership, and communication training to organizations, associations, and schools across North America, Europe, and Asia.

Jay received his Bachelor of Science degree from the United States Military Academy at West Point, with a concentration in Nuclear Physics.

From being a qualified Airborne/Ranger, Military Commander, Sales Professional, Corporate Manager, and Entrepreneur, Jay brings a unique background of interpersonal skills and business experience to each of his training and speaking engagements.

Within his community, Jay is and has been involved with numerous public service activities including a member of the Saratoga Springs City School District Board of Education, Board of Directors for Patriot Hills of New York, President of the Board for the Friends of the NYS Military Museum, a member of the 20th Congressional District Service Academy Selection Committee, and a columnist for the Saratogian newspaper.

He and his wife, Noni, have two adult children, Nicole and Jared.

Have Jay C. Rifenbary
Speak at Your Next Event

Jay C. Rifenbary's exciting, effective approach to motivation and leadership will provide the catalyst to higher levels of achievement and productivity for your company or organization.

Ideal for corporate, education, medical, association, sales, public service, and other enterprising industries, these one-of-a-kind programs will equip your employees with the tools they need to succeed.

- No Excuse! - Incorporating Core Values, Accountability and Balance into Your Life & Career
- No Excuse! - An Action Plan for Productive and Profitable Success
- No Excuse! - An Inspirational Approach to Enhancing Educational Accountability
- No Excuse! - An Accountable Approach to Unified Care and Patient Satisfaction
- No Excuse! - Building Industry Esprit and Team Unity
- No Excuse! - Igniting Sales Performance & Professionalism
- No Excuse! - An Ethical Approach Toward Public Service

Custom programs are also available to meet your organization's unique, immediate needs. For more information, contact us at:

Rifenbary Training & Development

12 Bog Meadow Run • Saratoga Springs, NY 12866
p. (518) 573-4709 • jay@rifenbary.com
WWW.RIFENBARY.COM

Visit

WWW.RIFENBARY.COM

*for more information regarding
Jay C. Rifenbary and his Core Value
Development Training.*